NOT JUST A MUM

The Practical Guide to Juggling Motherhood, Work and Life

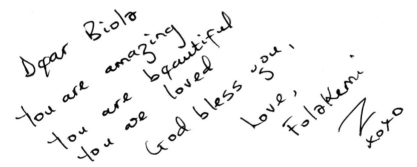

Folakemi Sebiotimo

First published in Great Britain 2018.

©Copyright Folakemi Sebiotimo.

All rights reserved. No part of this book may be reproduced, stored in a retrieval system, or transmitted by any means without the prior written permission of the author.

The right of Folakemi Sebiotimo to be identified as the author of this work has been asserted by her in accordance with the Copyright, Designs and Patents Act 1988.

Published by Amazon CreateSpace.

ISBN: 978-1-72183-143-2

Printed in the United Kingdom

Scripture taken from the HOLY BIBLE, NEW INTERNATIONAL VERSION®. NIV®. Copyright © 1973, 1978, 1984 by International Bible Society. Used by permission of Zondervan. All rights reserved worldwide.

Table of Contents

Dedication 1

Advance Praise for Not just a Mum 2

Meet the Contributors 5

The Paradigm Shift 7

Chapter One: Reassessing Purpose 17

Chapter Two: From Working Lady to Working Mum 47

Chapter Three: Standing Out at Work Sanely 84

Chapter Four: Organizing Your Home Life 125

Chapter Five: Work-Life Balance 141

Chapter Six: Building an Effective Support System 171

Chapter Seven: Self-Care and Self-Love 190

Chapter Eight: Putting Your Trust in God 229

Conclusion 247

References 253

Acknowledgements 255

About the Author 257

APPENDIX 258

Dedication

I would like to dedicate this book to all the busy but amazing and resilient working mums all over the world who are pushing through with their aspirations and interests despite the obstacles, are positive role models to their children, are building their homes and impacting their communities.

Advance Praise for Not just a Mum

It is so important that working mums everywhere share and celebrate the highs and lows of their experience, not just with fellow mums, but with all parents and non-parents alike. I'm so glad to read this honest and frank guide to taking one's authentic 'mum' self to work. It shows how being a working mum can be an asset for the career field, the family and the community.

- **Elly Hardwick, Managing Director, Global Head of Innovation, Deutsche Bank, and a mother of three children (United Kingdom)**

I would like to commend Folakemi for putting together this book, *Not Just a Mum*, an enlightening and educative book for working mums. Reading other peoples' insights from this book will make you realise that you are not alone in this journey and feel inspired by how they tackled some of the challenges that come with this joyful season. This is a great resource for busy mums who need to come to the realisation that they don't need to do everything but instead need to figure out how to prioritise what is important to them based on their circumstance and the season they are in. I will encourage every mum to get a copy of this book, as there are so many nuggets you can pick up from it.

- **Morenike Ajayi, Finance Director, author and founder of Career Nuggets and a mother of one child (United Kingdom)**

Firstly I must say this is a particularly outstanding piece that I enjoyed reading. It is a must have for every mum regardless of the age of their children. I believe, even grandmas will find it useful in terms of supporting their children and children in-law. Don't forget that they are getting younger and most are still working grandmas! Finally, I believe this is an original piece that will impact on women, men and grand parents alike. Really proud of you, Folakemi- I can't wait to lay hands on my copy.

-**Omotayo Adenuga, Senior Midwifery Lecturer, Pastor and a mother of two children (United Kingdom)**

As a very busy working mother to two fantastic boys, I have learnt from experience that with determination and the right support systems, it is possible to juggle both career and motherhood and find fulfilment without losing yourself. I would highly recommend this book to new mums and women who are at the verge of shelving their careers to focus solely on motherhood due to the frustration of finding the right balance.

- Hadiza Bala Usman, Managing Director, Nigerian Ports Authority, and a mother of two children (Nigeria)

Not Just a Mum is a must-read for any mum who wants to aim high and set the right standards for a good and balanced life, as well as for her children. It is packed with relatable tips and advice as it has been written from the author's life journey. It's also a very practical book with templates that can be easily adapted. I wish I had read this book whilst navigating through the early days of being a mum.

- Shola Alabi, Education Consultant, Centre Director and Founder of Raising Successful Children, and a mother of two children (United Kingdom)

Folakemi's book is a must-read even before you become a mum, but even more so if you are juggling work, children, and a partner, as it contains relevant tips on work-life balance and time management which any busy mum can relate to. One of the most important factors I could relate to when reading the book was the element of retaining part of your identity when you're a mum and continuing to nurture your talents, potential, and capabilities, not only for yourself but for your children who are watching you follow your dreams. It gives them permission to follow theirs. I hope those who read this book will take on the following message which Folakemi describes so beautifully; she states that you're 'not just a mum'—you are far more than that.

- Michele Attias, Life Coach, Speaker and Author of *Look Inside*, and a mother of two children (United Kingdom)

My motto in life as a thirty-something single and childless woman is certainly to do what I want when I want. However, even with the freedom to do as I please, my life is so busy and twenty-four hours a day is often not enough. This book has inspired me to really think about the things that I hold dear and make a plan now for when I have children to ensure that I can still do the things I love, have a productive career, and love and care for my children. Ultimately, having children should never be the end of one's lifelong dreams, goals, or ambitions. This book really reinforces and guides you to identify what work-life balance means to you. It is a must-read for future mums.

- Zainab Atta, Vice President, Financial Crime Assurance, and future Mother (United Kingdom)

This book is brilliantly laid out and it inspired me a lot. A must-read for all mothers who are ready to live out their dreams while raising a wholesome family.

-Bunmi Olabode- Project Manager and a mother of three children (Nigeria)

Finally... a relevant book filled with insightful stories, practical tips, and everyday strategies for a new generation of passionate women who refuse to give up on their dreams.

-Jokotade Adeniyi, International Artist, Entrepreneur, Speaker and a mother of two children (United States)

Meet the Contributors

1. **Tolulope Adedeji**- Marketing Director, entrepreneur, mum of four, Nigeria
2. **Gbemi Alabi**- Accountant, property expert, mum of one, United Kingdom
3. **Dr Monica Alabi**- Medical Doctor, healthcare leader, mum of three, United Kingdom
4. **Ifeyinwa Anthony**- Lawyer, entrepreneur, mum of five, Nigeria
5. **Saude Atoyebi**- Civil Servant, entrepreneur, mum of one, Nigeria
6. **Olamide Ayodele**- Project Manager, talk show host, mum of two, United Kingdom
7. **Annabelle Baiyewu**- Entrepreneur, mum of two, United Kingdom
8. **Bimbola Banjo-Osagie**- Business Analyst, Property Investor, podcaster, mum of four, United Kingdom
9. **Melinda Barthel**- Lead Business Analyst, mum of two, United Kingdom
10. **Kayla Dene**- Entrepreneur, mum of one, United States
11. **Funmilola Famodimu**- HR Manager, mum of two, Nigeria
12. **Abosede George-Ogan**- Director of Strategy, Funding, and Stakeholder Management, author, mum of three, Nigeria
13. **Elizabeth French**- Programme Manager, mum of two, United Kingdom
14. **Kiki Gillman**- Lawyer, Fitness Coach, mum of three, United States
15. **Abby Imafidion**- Accountant, mum of one, United Kingdom
16. **Lara Nassar Imseeh**- Research Fellow, mum of one, Jordan
17. **Melanie Kakuli**- Nurse, wedding planner, mum of one, Canada
18. **Lola Komolafe**- Fitness Coach (April Laugh), mum of one, United Kingdom

19. **Omolade Lawal**- Kumon Instructor, mum of two, Australia
20. **Sunny Li**- Business Analyst, fitness enthusiast, mum of two, United Kingdom
21. **Jo Maxwell**- IT Consultant, talk show host, Founder of Passionate Empowered Women Network, mum of three, United Kingdom
22. **Kelly Nevin**- eLearning Manager, mum of one, United Kingdom
23. **Glory Ojuyenum**- Client Services, events planner, mum of three, United Kingdom
24. **Feyi Olubokun**- Executive Assistant, mum of one, Dubai UAE
25. **Abi Olukeye**- Global Product Manager, Founder and Creative Director of Raising Smart Girls, mum of two, United States
26. **Olivia Onasanya**- Project Manager, Investment Banking, mum of four, United Kingdom
27. **Emma Reed**- Lifestyle/Parenting blogger and author, mum of two, United Kingdom
28. **Dr Bibiana Yetty**- Dentist, YouTube vlogger, mum of three, United Kingdom

The Paradigm Shift

At the age of twenty-four, I landed my "dream job" as Application Developer (software engineer) at a top global investment bank, Deutsche Bank, in the vibrant city of London. I was single and had just completed a master's degree in information systems at the University of Sheffield after completing a bachelor's degree in computer science. I was a very ambitious, self-driven, and goal-oriented young woman. Being born and raised in Nigeria (West Africa) meant my aspirations and standards, when it came to my education and career, were extremely high from a very young age. If I were second place in my class, my mum (who was a school teacher back then) would ask me, "Does the person who came first have two heads?"

When I started working in London in 2009, my goal was to become a vice president before the age of thirty-two. I travelled to India and New York on business trips and flew first class within six months of joining the firm. I was a top performer at work. Within my first year at the firm, I was the department's sole recipient of the Recognizing and Rewarding Achievement award, which involved receiving a monetary gift and a congratulatory phone call from the chief information officer. The sky definitely seemed just like a starting point at the time.

After I got married in early 2012, things started to change for me. My drive, passion, and self-motivation began to take a back-seat and. When my first son was born in 2013, my focus and priorities suddenly changed. The vibrant, fun, and adventurous life I had before getting married and having children no longer existed. The question I always asked myself was, "What happened to that carefree twenty-three-year-old that could book an impromptu girl trip to Paris over the bank holiday weekend?" The same girl who could effortlessly give a technical roadmap presentation to a room full of people?" I mean, I had jumped off a moving plane at over eight thousand feet somewhere in Oxford to raise money for charity, so where did all that passion and confidence suddenly go?

The Tipping Point

Upon returning to work, after being on maternity leave for a year, I really struggled to adapt to working life while juggling my life as a working mum. My confidence took a hit, and suddenly, I could barely speak up in meetings. I second-guessed most of my work deliveries because I didn't feel confident anymore. I recall a few occasions where I would go to the office bathroom to have a cry.

On the home front, things were not going well either. My son and I both fell ill the second week I returned to work. My husband was working outside London in Surrey, which meant his commute was two and a half hours each way. I had a weekday nanny, an elderly woman who tried very hard to meet most of my childcare expectations. I had no family around to help and some days I was so stressed because everything that could have gone wrong pretty much did so. All I could do was keep putting one foot in front of the other, praying that God would get me through while tears streamed down my face.

Before this time, I had never suffered with persistent sadness, irritability, depression, or anxiety. I felt so overwhelmed, continually unhappy, and guilty. I had a poor appetite, I lost a lot of weight, and I was constantly tired. I spoke to an office-based therapist after I went back into work but was never officially diagnosed. However, based on my symptoms, it was very clear that I suffered from an extended Post-Natal Depression (PND). At that time, I couldn't see the light at the end of the tunnel.

It wasn't until that fateful morning train commute to work that I had a sudden realization: I was going to lose my self-motivated, passionate, vibrant, and happy self if I didn't make some serious lifestyle changes. I already had so many reasons to be happy. I had a reasonably good husband, a delightful son, and I lived and worked in one of my favourite cities in the world. Most of my family was in Nigeria and the United States but I had started to make some good supportive friends in London. I was in good health. Despite all my blessings, I was still often unhappy because I let the transition from being a working girl to a working mum take a huge toll on me. I felt my husband was not providing enough hands-on support at home. I became a wife who constantly nagged. On the commute that day, I finally figured out my goal in life was simply to be happy—whatever that meant.

I realised I had to do something. I could survive no longer without resetting my expectations and prioritising what mattered to me. I made a few important changes to my life, thanks to the great support system I connected with. First, I found a great live-in nanny. Then I changed roles to another department in the workplace; I "leaned in" for a bit and pushed for my assistant vice president promotion, which I got within a year. I also decided to bring back that fun-loving woman who liked to laugh so much and have fun. Motherhood didn't mean my life should come to an end. I started attending concerts, girlfriend dinners, the cinema, and massage dates—things I did before I had children—with my close mum friends. I set aside time for bible study and devotion. I read just about every book or article I could get my hands on relating to parenting, early years foundation, and work-life balance. I even asked more experienced mums for advice on how to implement strategies to maintain a healthy work-life balance.

The *Notjustamum* blog (rebranded as *Peacockscanfly,* www.peacockscanfly.com) community was born out of my desire to network and connect with other like-minded, passionate, and "cool" mums.

Through the years, I have tried a variety of different systems in my home and workplace to bring some order and definitive enjoyment. Some things worked; others didn't. Amid the joyful chaos, my second son was born, and we were a family of four. I guess I just want you to understand that I get it. I have never lived in a perfect world; nor do I aim to. I believe it's important for mums to be real with each other. However, reality means that life can sometimes be hard, chaotic, messy, and stressful.

Over time, I'll say about three years into being a mum and after fully settling back into work and being able to cope reasonably well with life as a busy working mum, I eventually became the mum who inspired others. I was constantly being told that I was a super mum and was always put together in every sense.

Why Did I Write this Book?

When I had my first baby in 2013, I didn't know what I was doing so I just went with the flow. I didn't know much about what it takes to be a working mum in the 21st century especially when you have limited local support because you migrated away from your country of origin. I joined Netmums and Baby Centre, which are both great platforms to connect with other mums around the world. But I couldn't find any relevant platform or book tailored to new working mums with a limited support system. So, I read every book or article I could find relating to parenting, career, work-life balance, and faith. I also started my lifestyle blog and created a Facebook group for like-minded mums. These allowed me to connect with many other mums from all over the world in similar situations. This book consolidates my research, and I hope to inspire other working mums by sharing experiences and insights from others about what worked or didn't work. There is no such thing as perfect parenting; it simply does not exist. In this book, I hope to provide useful and practical tips to make your life as a working mum easier.

What is Different About This Book?
One thing that makes this book different is that I am communicating to you from a place of experience. I have experienced it all and I am still experiencing the highs, lows and struggles working mums with young children face, especially those with a limited support system.

Most of my strong family ties were still in Nigeria, meaning I had very little family support in the United Kingdom.

I have a busy job I need to commute to daily, grocery shopping to do, cooking, cleaning, washing dishes, laundry, school runs, limited childcare options, attending school functions, homework, children's' activities, and importantly, making time for my husband. This is the real world. Many working mums, me included, feel there is no end to the to-do lists and not enough time available for chasing our other passions, relaxing, or making time for ourselves.

When I was in the process of finding a new nanny and my husband was working away from home, I had to discipline, encourage, and manage activities for the children all by myself whilst still going to work. One night I was so knackered that I collapsed in bed in my work clothes without any dinner, utterly exhausted. The worst of it all was that I woke up the next day to the same problems, the same issues, and the same imperfections. So, trust me when I say I get it. I want to offer you real encouragement and advice.

Motherhood is unique to each family, and no one can say you are doing it wrong.

Furthermore, I have incorporated the experiences and perspectives of several working mums from all over the world—the United Kingdom, Canada, Nigeria, Jordan, the United States, and United Arab Emirates and Australia. These women are from various career and business backgrounds, including investment banking, finance, law, technology, healthcare, and transport. I crowd-sourced for extra tips to capture a broader perspective and make the book more relevant.

I have discovered an effective approach to becoming a highly efficient and successful mum, regardless of your personal circumstances. Since becoming a mum more than five years ago, I have read many parenting and inspirational books but have found there is limited literary material tailored specifically to new working mums, young mums, future mums, and mums that migrated away from where they were born and raised. Connecting with working mums through various channels such as local baby and children's groups, church, work, and social media has encouraged me to see that one can share inspiring and practical experiences and insights on the infinite ways we can be 'great' and successful mothers, despite the constant challenges and impediments. What I can't stress enough is that I would not be able to cope with the challenges of being a working mum without my Christian faith. In short, I want to help other mums in similar positions and hope that my experiences can aid others to navigate their way through life as a working mum.

Intended Audience

The target audience includes working mums, mums-to-be, new mums, young mums, future mums in the junior to middle management career and job level, mums with a limited support system, and mums that migrated to another country without much local support. My research shows the greatest need of my target audience is TIME. They all wish they could add an extra hour or two to a day. Other challenges relate to achieving the work-life balance, coping with juggling work, family, and passions, knowing what to do, and when and how to prioritise the challenges associated with childcare. I also believe this guide will benefit the more experienced mums who have older children.

More than half of the mums who took part in the research phase are working mums from the United Kingdom and from the Technology and Banking sector; however, I believe any mum or woman can learn from and adapt to some of the practical tips in this narration.

This book is a practical guide and I believe Christian mums will benefit the most, as many of the resulting themes related to perseverance and grace are due to my values being greatly influenced by my Christian faith.

Scope and Assumptions

This book assumes the working mum has a supportive spouse or partner to share the load with. I feel like there would be a need to write a different practical guide solely for single working mums with limited local support as their challenges would be hugely different. My working mum experience is based on being a girl with African roots and values but has been immensely influenced by western culture which I would have imbibed knowingly or unknowingly through migrating to the United Kingdom.

I see a lot of new or inexperienced mums providing all sorts of advice in books and on the internet for issues which they have very little experience in themselves. As my children are only in pre-school and year one right now, I would not be the right person to write about advice on how to combine work with raising older school-age children, tweens, or teens. I'm not there yet.

Many of the insights which are based on a mum being on a professional career path can also be applied to mums in business and entrepreneurs. This book reflects a small group of working mums' experiences, opinions, and perspectives. Each section of this book contains insights from real working mums who are all great examples in their own unique and individual way. The best advice is to listen to those who have gone ahead of you successfully, or who seem to have figured it out, and then determine what works for you. Not everything in this book will resonate with you and that is fine. However, I encourage you to read every section with an open mind and jot down what is applicable or useful to you.

Discrimination against working mums is still widespread in today's modern society; however, this book is not intended to be about what is broken in our social order. The decision to be a parent is based on choice and, although it may be in society's best interest to accommodate our choices, it is not society's responsibility to accommodate them. In the past, many working parents figured out how to raise children successfully and then just got on with it.
There are many other topics I would love to write about. However, I can't cover them all in one book due to the publisher imposed word-limit. I will like to share my childhood journey and what it was like growing up in Nigeria. I would like to write about my work experiences coping in a heavily male dominated workplace. It will be beneficial to shed more light on the gender pay gap in the corporate world—focusing on junior and mid-level management female professionals. I would love to write about the challenges new working mums and hard-working black immigrants like me face in the United Kingdom. When

immigrants enter a western society, they can encounter a web of prejudice blocking their path to success and their well-being. Based on my experiences, it's obvious that black immigrants would have a harder time getting and keeping a highly paid specialist job. Furthermore, a high proportion of immigrant mums have to bear the double expectation of building new communities and support systems while simultaneously maintaining their home country's culture and values in the new world.

This book is not a parenting book; it simply provides practical advice based on what has worked for me in my journey as a working mum with limited local support. If you need an accurate parenting book, renowned child psychologist Laura Markham's book *Calm Parents, Happy Kids: The Secrets of Stress-Free Parenting* is one I would highly recommend.

This book is not about marriage. I am still learning every day how to work as a team with my husband to get good results in our home and relationship; we are a work in progress. If you need recommendations for good faith-based marriage literature, I would highly recommend *Marriage as God Intended* by Selwyn Hughes and *The Five Love Languages: The Secret to Love that Lasts* by Gary Chapman.

I continue to struggle with work, motherhood, marriage, and faith daily; I don't have it all put together all the time, but I ask God for help daily and I am always willing to learn new and exciting ways of doing things. However, on a positive note, I am now in a place where I can start to regain confidence and I am finding my own rhythm and approach. I hope you enjoyed this peek into my life as I transformed from working girl to working mum. Perhaps you'll be motivated by how I dealt with some of the challenges I faced. My hope is that you will find inspiration and encouragement in the insights and perspectives from mums all over the world who are doing a range of work in addition to raising their children, including working full-time, part-time, freelancing, and running their own businesses.

Terminologies

- Mom and mum are used interchangeably throughout this book and mean the same thing, an informal word for mother and a person who gives birth to or adopts a child.
- Spouse and husband are used interchangeably and refer to a male partner in a marriage.
- Nursery and day care are used interchangeably and refer to care provided during the day for young children to allow their parents to work.
- 'Not just a mum' is a multi-passionate woman and mother who wears many hats and fulfils multiple roles within her family and community. She is strong, confident, loving, smart, a go-getter, solution-focused, and is not afraid of being her authentic self. Apart from being a mum, she could also be a sister, wife, aunt, friend, colleague, entrepreneur, or mentor.
- A 'working mum' is a person who engages in work or business activities for income, in addition to her duties as a childcare provider.

Chapter One: Reassessing Purpose

The mystery of human existence lies not in just staying alive but finding something to live for. — **Fyodor Dostoyevsky**

When I started working in London ten years ago, I often had to work overtime at the office in Bishopsgate to fix issues with the Equity trading application I supported at the time. Working late wasn't really a problem then, as I was young, free, and single and had no major responsibilities or commitments outside of work. Besides, my flat was a short twenty-minute bus ride from the office. I could go for a night out after work in Shoreditch until 11pm without worrying too much about responsibilities apart from what to eat for dinner.

My main life goals in my early twenties, before I got married and started having children, were to very quickly climb the corporate ladder, volunteer for suitable causes, and travel the world. My top career aspiration was to become a vice president before the age of thirty-two. I once arrived at the office at

9:20am straight from an early Monday morning flight back from Alicante, Spain, suitcase in tow. I immediately jumped into our 9:30am daily stand-up project meeting with not a hair out of place. I was very dedicated and committed to my job. I often went on business trips to India to train our offshore development team on the use of new technology. I was my department's sole recipient of a RARE (Recognizing and Rewarding Excellence) award. The sky seemed to be my starting point.

I was a regular volunteer at the Whitechapel mission, a charity which provides support to the homeless. Some of my volunteering activities included cooking and serving breakfast to the homeless, providing guidance and advice on night shelters, hostels, benefits, and form filing, and helping them find appropriate help.

At that time, I had a bucket list of thirty items to do before I turned thirty. The top five items on my list were:

- Sky diving and bungee jumping
- Buy a property
- Throwing a fundraiser for a faith-based or charitable cause
- Visit thirty countries
- Train for a marathon

Obviously, life became increasingly complicated when I got married and had children. I became more committed to my job and family and have less free time to follow my passions. It becomes progressively difficult and expensive to make plans and travel. I had a strong sense of purpose before having children, but, I had to re-define my purpose in life and set new realistic and achievable goals after having children.

Many are the plans in a person's heart, but it is the Lord's purpose that will prevail. **Proverbs 19:12**

Today, I am a married and working mum of two young children. Whilst I have not yet done bungee jumping, trained for a proper marathon or visited thirty countries, I am very blessed and thank God for where I am in my life. I still work in technology within the investment banking sector (currently four days a week on a 9-5 schedule).

I have worked part-time, full-time, and remotely in the five years since I became a working mum. I have not attained the vice president corporate title yet however my performance reviews at work have remained positive given how much my productivity level increased. I also run a lifestyle website and mums' online group. I am a fitness enthusiast. I love travelling. I volunteer for church activities and in general. I am a career mentor. I have been to UK schools to give talks about my career to pupils and students. I have facilitated Speed Careers Day for GCSE students and have also worked as a STEMette mentor (Science Technology Engineering and Mathematics), a scheme that encourages young girls to explore STEM degrees and careers. So, I know first-hand the challenges and difficulties associated with pursuing your passion while raising young children.

Thankfully, I have support from my husband, a good weekday nanny, day care, and school. Every minute I'm not with my children, I'm either working, running errands, or pursuing my passions. But I'm not complaining, as I wouldn't have it any other way. I am not where I hoped to be in my career nevertheless I am very grateful to God that I still have a relatively flexible but interesting 9-5 corporate job that has allowed me to continue pursuing my writing and other passions.

As a young girl aged seven growing up in Nigeria, I saw my mother who was a very good school teacher try to be successful in business. Alongside her job as a teacher, she sourced and imported several women's fashion items and sold them at her own shop. Sometimes some of her business activities were successful and other times she took huge losses. Many of her clients were friends and family who on many occasions owed her so much money and never paid back. But she didn't give up. Watching her drive and significant efforts in her career and business over the years made me into the multi-passionate woman I am today.

Since I became a working mum in 2013, I have had to find a new 'normal' for the dreamer and go-getter in me. I'm not going to lie, keeping a job and pursuing your passions while raising children can be very hard. I have to be intentional if I want to follow through with my goals. I have to plan, re-plan, and be more organised. I have to rely heavily on my husband. I have to use the help of trusted and supportive people. I understand that I cannot do everything on my own. I have to ask God for help. Not only do I need encouragement and support from my family, friends and mentors, I also need practical help with childcare.

You might have a sickly or special needs child which could make it harder to keep a job, find a job, or do anything outside of being a parent. Pursuing your dream is tough; pursuing it with children is even tougher. You might be overwhelmed and feel like giving up because the children have behavioural issues or they are not doing well in school, and those are valid reasons to take time out from your career. However, you have to recognise the difference between taking time out, reducing your working hours, and leaving all together.

I have been tempted to 'hide' behind my children several times. I wanted to quit my day job many times when it got too hard. I wanted to quit my writing many times when I felt overwhelmed. I missed my maternity leave days when I could spend so much time with the children. Thankfully, I have great mentors that encourage me to keep going when times get tough. Trust me, there are no medals for sacrificing your dreams altogether for your children. Instead, you might wake up one day and totally resent yourself.

Children tend to make it harder for you to follow your dreams, but they usually make it so much more rewarding. Sometimes children make us change our purpose and dreams and that is not always a bad thing. However, we need to stop using the children as an excuse for quitting on our dreams.

So, why should you continue to follow your dreams after having children?

- It's important to retain part of your identity and independence when you're a mum. One of the scariest things for me when I first became a mum was being unsure about how I could still be myself. I was very worried I would become more 'mum' than 'me'.
- Each one of you has been created with unique special talents and abilities. It is necessary for you to continue running with the things which have been put inside of you.
- It is fulfilling and rewarding to meet some of your set goals. It is also nice to follow other passions that have a tangible end, ones where you can see results from your actions.

- You want my children to grow up watching you follow your dreams. You want them to know that even when life gets tough and chaotic, it's still possible to carry on. When your children watch you succeed, it will show them that they can follow their dreams and help them aspire for great things.
- I want my children to talk about my accomplishments to their friends. I want to show them what it looks like for a woman to pursue her dreams and passions audaciously. I want to raise them to become caring hands-on men that will lean in and support their wives' dreams in the future.

What is Your Why?

A goal should scare you a little and excite you a lot. —Joe Vitale

I ask that you take a step back - regardless of where you are in your career or motherhood journey. Now think carefully about these questions: What makes you tick? Why do you do what you do? What has been pressed in your heart to achieve? What makes you want to get out of bed every day? What are you interested in? When do you feel most at peace?

Why am I asking you to reflect on your *Why?* Because a clear sense of purpose enables you to focus your efforts and time on what matters to you the most. It will help you say NO to things that do not matter to you and to stay motivated when the chips are down, compelling you to take risks and push forward regardless of the obstacles or setbacks.

A big factor in finding your purpose is also recognizing what you're good at. The most successful people are constantly obsessed with solving an important problem, something that matters to them.

Your *Why* is usually something bigger than you. Your purpose can change over time especially after a life-changing event, like becoming a mum.

I have always been a multi-passionate woman, but it was not until after I became a mum that I explicitly asked myself this question: "What is my Why?" I had to pray to God to find out exactly what my purpose in life is; after all, he was the one who created me.

One of the messages I clearly heard was to use my writing and my voice to empower, inspire, and motivate women, and this is certainly my biggest life calling. It all made sense because over the years I have found that women are usually drawn to me for inspiration relating to career, fashion, style, motherhood, food, travel…you name it. I have organized way too many parties and events in my lifetime.

Let me share with you my own *Why*, re-defined after I became a mum. "I love being a mum and wife because it allowed me to find my God-given passion and purpose in life. I love to solve problems, improve and simplify processes for organisations and individuals across all areas. I am passionate about empowering individuals (women in particular) to make choices which will optimise their personal, professional, business, or spiritual growth, allowing them to live their best life."

Write Down Your *Why*

It's important to re-establish your *Why* based on your current circumstances. Write it down.

What Does Motherhood Mean to You?

Motherhood in its simplest form, means to give birth, adopt children, be the sole carer of children, and to make a family. But being a mother is also about much more than that. It is something huge and sometimes overwhelming.

For me, motherhood means finally knowing the value of true, unconditional love and having a reason to look forward to tomorrow. It means putting your children's needs above your own from the point of conception until the day you die. It's hard, and sometimes thankless, but it is always worthwhile. Yes, there are difficult times where you count down the minutes, if not seconds, before bedtime, or when you bite your tongue not to lash out verbally at your children. Motherhood is a roller coaster ride of ups and downs, joys and fears, but in the end it is worth the ride.

An important question to ask yourself, even before becoming a mum, is how you feel about motherhood in the first place. I wish I had asked myself this question before I became a mum. All I knew then was that I loved children, especially babies, because they looked very cute.

Make sure your husband or partner is ready financially, emotionally, and mentally. You cannot do this alone and, ideally, you should not do this alone. A child should be a happy gift to the both of you. Therefore, plan it.
Lara, mum of one

MUMMY'S CORNER

What does motherhood mean to you?

Caregiving is the true meaning of motherhood. Carrying a child in your womb is one thing, but taking care of them is a different story. Motherhood is both rewarding and challenging at the same time. You are constantly juggling with emotional and practical demands. That is why I spend time in prayer, meditating the word of God for wisdom and strength.

Melanie, mum of one

It is a blessing, an act of loving unconditionally and putting the welfare of my child first.

Gbemi, mum of one

To me, motherhood means being selfless, patient, and kind. I can pray and hope for my daughter every day but, at some point, she is going to discover herself and I want to give her the freedom to do that. I want her to form her own opinions, dreams, and style. Motherhood is a superpower and I feel like it has its stages from new-born to adulthood. There is the learning and teaching stage (new-born), the disciplinary and having-a-lot-of-faith stage (teenage years), and the friendship stage (adulthood).

Kayla, mum of one

Motherhood means putting my child first, above everything in this world. I will lay down my life in a second for her. Motherhood means not buying the latest designer handbag but buying expensive baby clothes that she outgrows within six months. Watching children's TV and enjoying it. It's about making new friends with other parents at the preschool gate. Finally, motherhood is wanting another baby after a very difficult first pregnancy and the feelings of disappointment when it's not happening.

Abby, mum of one

For me, motherhood is being selfless and putting someone else's needs above yours. It is loving someone so much you will give up anything and everything for that person. Motherhood is making mistakes and learning from them. Motherhood is the unconditional love that my daughters show me. No matter what's going on, I look into their eyes and all I see is love and the pure adoration for me. (Well, at least while they are still so young.)

Annabelle, mum of two

Motherhood for me started unexpectedly when I was twenty. I had my first son, then it was much easier to cope and do things working around one schedule. After having the last two, it's a bit more challenging but I would not change a thing. I love being a mum. It's funny because I can't imagine my life any other way anymore.

Glory, mum of three

Motherhood to me is synonymous with unconditional love, protection, and nurture for another being who is a part of me and whom I am a part of. I believe that children are custodians of our legacy and through them we have a form of immortality.

Olamide, mum of one

Motherhood to me is a myriad of things. It's about sacrifice, joy, tiredness, strength, and pure guts. It's about stretching yourself, lateral thinking, and being observant. I can say that being a mum has made me a better person. It has made me more patient, happier, stronger and I've discovered things about myself I didn't know, like my ability to run efficiently on little to no sleep when I have a new-born and other children to handle! It's a rollercoaster and I genuinely am grateful for it.

Ifeyinwa, mum of five

Being a Mum does not Define Me

Motherhood is a glorious gift but do not define yourself solely by motherhood. —Chimamanda Adichie

Motherhood is the greatest blessing as established, however it does not fully define my identity. Motherhood is one aspect of my identity, yes. My children are the centre of my day-to-day schedule because I must first consider them before I make any decision in my life. Motherhood has made me into a better version of myself and has allowed me discover and accept my real self. But I am also a woman, a Christian, a daughter, a sister, a wife, a friend, an aunt, a sister-in-law, a daughter-in-law, an employee, a writer, a blogger, a Nigerian citizen, a UK citizen, a mentor, a fitness enthusiast, Instagram addict, and several other things. This world is vast and it has countless experiences to offer in our short lifetime. Without a doubt out of all these aspects of my life, my children are the favourite part and the title of mother is the one I am most proud of. Being a mother is what fulfils me the most.

The Benefits of Being a Working Mum

She considers a piece of land and buys it; out of her earnings she plants a vineyard. —Proverbs 31:16

Women have been giving birth and working since the beginning of time. In the past, and in some modern cultures, they had the baby in a field and went straight back to work. Even in cultures where women didn't work, historically, they were usually responsible for managing the finances of the household because they were better at it. 2017 Families and Labour market statistics from the Office of National Statistics (ONS) suggests there are about 75% of women with dependent children in work. Most mums either working from home or from an office (or a mixture), part-time or full-time, usually need to work to provide for their family or want to work because they are intelligent, smart, and talented. Proverbs 31:16 is my biggest inspiration for being a strong and smart working mum. Many women work to support their family financially to give their children a better life, self-fulfilment, self-esteem, identity, a stronger sense of purpose, adult interaction, social connections. Harvard researchers found that working mums have more successful daughters and caring sons. McGinn (2018). The study was conducted in twenty-four countries and advocates that daughters of working mothers have better careers, higher pay, and more equal relationships than those who had stay-at-home mothers when they grew up. Furthermore, their sons thrive and grow up to be better men, getting more involved at home and taking extra time over caring for their families than their counterparts.

I asked eight working mothers why they choose to go back to work after having their children. Here are their responses:

- *Hot tea and the option to go to the toilet alone.*
- *I needed interaction and going back to work was the best thing. I like being me rather than mum all the time.*
- *Simply because I made more money than my husband and decided to go back.*
- *I enjoy my job and I want to raise my children to think they can have careers and kids if they want.*
- *It gives us the money to travel together more often which is what I love to do.*
- *I needed the money and being at home was driving me crazy.*
- *For my sanity and self-care. What I want is important too.*

- *A self-employed husband means I am the one with the regular stable income and I would hate to have to rely on someone else for money.*

The Realities of Being a Working Mum

You constantly feel like an average mum, an average employee, an average wife, an average daughter, an average sister, or an average friend. You want to give 100% in everything you do but it never happens because you're spread too thin.

Whether you work because you have a passion for your job or you work because you can't afford not to, the decision to become a working mum is personal and one that only you can make. A working mother should feel proud of herself, as she has the power to give her best to her family whilst at the same time not forgetting her responsibilities. Remember, you're not alone. There are tons of working mums and parents out there with similar challenges and struggles and everyone is doing an awesome job. Know that someday you and your children will look back and be proud of everything you have accomplished.

Which of these realities can you relate to?

- You could miss out on important milestones such as first steps, first words, and important school meetings and events due to work commitments, which can cause feelings of guilt.
- Time spent with your children will be precious and a privilege rather than a necessity.

- Your calendar might have recurring appointments for swimming lessons, football, ballet, karate, music class, and kid parties. Your social life outside of work could become non-existent.
- You may have numerous opportunities to interact with other adults, whether they are colleagues, bosses, or clients, and hold intellectual conversation during the working day. You might get to engage in social activities like team drinks, office parties, business meetings, and corporate outings.
- The satisfaction of doing a good job, putting on smart office clothes, and feeling like you are living a purpose-driven life for yourself as well as your family can boost self-esteem and confidence.
- A good work day can feel like a vacation from the constant chaos and demands of motherhood.
- You might work part-time and be expected to deliver like a full-time employee.
- You could end up constantly exhausted and resentful, especially if you don't have a supportive husband to share the household duties with.
- It may be difficult to advance in your career due to less time to commit to work.

Identify Your Career and Family Goals

Setting your goals is the first step in turning the invisible into the visible.
—Tony Robbins

We have established what motherhood means, why you are more than a mum, why it's important for women to work, the realities of being a working mum, and that being a working mum should not have any impact on your child's development. Still, to be a good mother means putting our children's needs before your own. So how can we put our children's needs first and still have a successful career? Doesn't a successful career mean putting in long hours? How can we say we're putting our children's needs before ours when we're not always there for them?

Knowing what you want is the first step toward getting it. —Mae West.

The first step you can take toward becoming the parent, mother, wife, and/or employee you want to be is to define what that means to you. This can begin with a process of defining and writing your goals and values down and then putting them into action, with periodic reviews to see whether you are moving toward your goals or not.

After having children, you will need to realign and refocus your career aspirations and determine how they will work with your parenting vision and overall purpose in life. You will need to sit down with your spouse to develop a clear picture of what your goals are as a family particularly what your combined values are for raising your children. Then you should start with setting meaningful periodic goals. The biggest thing I have learnt is that your spouse is your greatest asset and he can either make or break you. If your fundamental values and beliefs are not aligned, setting a common family goal could prove hugely challenging.

Likewise, as an employee and especially after having children, you will need to re-define your career goals. Do you want to become a team leader in two years? Articulate it and be realistic with your set timelines. Do you want to learn about a new business area? Write it down.

In the book *The Seven Habits of Highly Effective People: Powerful Lessons in Personal Change*, Steven Covey highlights the importance of having a personal mission statement that articulates the values that represent you as a person.

You need to think deeply about what is important to you in the short and long term and how you can make it all work. Here are some questions new working parents and parents-to-be should ask to determine what is important:

- Where would you like to be in your career in the short (six months to two years), medium (three to five years) and long term (over five years)?
- What is your vision for your children and family in five years' time? In ten years?
- What are the most important values you want to pass on to your children?
- What skills do you want to nurture in your children? Examples are self-esteem, hard work, curiosity, confidence, compassion, and determination.
- What would be the definition of success for your children?
- How would you like your children to describe what it was like growing up with you as a parent?

Once you understand what motherhood means to you and you've identified what your short and long-term career goals are, you need to define a vision that will enable you to synchronise it with your overall career and parenting goals. A vision statement describes what your ideal family life would look like and how it links to your career goals. It will provide inspiration for what you hope to achieve in five, ten, or even fifteen to twenty years. It helps you understand how your career will ultimately contribute towards accomplishing your family goals in the long term.

Create a SMART Goal Statement

Most people spend a great amount of time and effort trying to find their purpose and equilibrium in life. It becomes a constant battle to achieve a decent work-life balance, forever chasing to get a pay rise or promotion, trying to get more clients for one's business, attempting to lose weight or keep physically fit, and, in most cases, people spread themselves too thin. They find themselves in a constant loop of trying to do everything and anything while accomplishing very little.

If you want to live a happy life, tie it to a purpose, not to people or things.
— Albert Einstein

When I returned to my corporate job in 2014 after having been on maternity leave for a year, I found I was becoming less happy with my life. I was inundated with the pressures of a demanding job on top of experiencing working-mum guilt whilst trying to balance the transition from being a working lady to becoming a working mum. After hitting rock bottom, I finally figured out that my overall objective in life is to simply...

Enjoy Every Moment

You can have simple goal statements for different phases and stages in your life. There is no right or wrong approach when it comes to creating and setting a career, business, or parenting goal. Using the SMART concept can help you focus on goal setting and setting yourself up for success. **SMART**, an acronym commonly attributed to the Peter Drucker's Management by Objectives concept, is widely used to guide goal setting. I have used the SMART concept in the last nine years to set annual goals, objective statements, and performance reviews at work.

SMART goal statements provide direction and purpose. They aim to steer you toward goals that are simple, measurable, achievable, relevant, and time bound (short-term and long-term). Setting SMART goals means you can clarify your ideas, focus your efforts, use your time and resources productively, and increase your chances of achieving what you want in life. The key advantages of SMART goals are that they are easier to understand and you know when they have been fulfilled.

SMART stands for:

Specific
Measurable
Achievable (Attainable)
Relevant (Realistic)
Time bound (Timely)

SPECIFIC

Focus is a matter of deciding on what things you're not going to do. —John Carmack

What is the goal and why is this goal important to you? Your goal should target a specific objective or area for improvement and should be simple, sensible, significant, and stretching. Find SPECIFIC answers to questions related to

What, Why, and How. Some questions to ask yourself when setting goals and objectives are:

- What exactly do I want to achieve?
- Why do I want to achieve this goal?
- How do I intend to achieve this goal?
- What are the limitations and obstacles that might prevent me from achieving this goal?
- What are possible alternative ways of achieving the same goal?

Example: Imagine you are a project support officer and a mum of children aged two and four. You have just returned from maternity leave and you would like to become a Project Manager. A **SPECIFIC** goal could be: I want to gain the skills and experience necessary to become a Project Manager within my organization's Client onboarding department or seek suitable external opportunities so that I can progress to the next stage of my career.

MEASURABLE

You cannot manage what you don't measure.

Your set goal should be quantifiable, or at least suggest an indicator of progress to stay focused and motivated. Your goals should be measurable, so you have tangible evidence that you have indeed accomplished it. This can be through setting smaller measurements incorporated into an overall goal. A measurable goal should address questions such as how much? How many? How will I know when it is accomplished?

Example: You might measure your goal of acquiring the skills to become a Project Manager by determining that you will have completed the necessary training courses such as PMP, PRINCE2, or an MSc in Project Management within a six-month time frame. Your measure of progress for acquiring the new skills could look like this: *Within the next six months, I intend to undertake a Project Management training course that would enable me to acquire the PRINCE2 practitioner qualification.*

The key measure in this example is whether you have attained a Project Management PRINCE2 qualification within six months.

ACHIEVABLE/ATTAINABLE

It always seems impossible until it is done. —Nelson Mandela

Your goal needs to be attainable based on known constraints and available resources. Goals should be achievable and they can stretch beyond your comfort zone so that you feel challenged. However, they should be defined well enough so that you can achieve them. You must possess or aim to attain appropriate skills, knowledge, and the abilities needed to achieve the goal or you will be more likely to fail. That doesn't mean you can't take on something that seems impossible and make it happen by planning smartly and going for it. An achievable goal will usually answer questions such as:

- How can I accomplish this goal?
- How realistic is the goal based on other constraints, such as financial circumstances or time?

Example

You might need to ask yourself whether developing the skills required to become a Project Manager is achievable based on your existing experience and qualifications. For example, given you have two young children, would you have time to complete the required training and coursework effectively? Can you afford to pay for the training courses? Write down all known obstacles that might prevent you from achieving your goals and write down mitigation actions for each obstacle.

An example of an obstacle could be: the ability to set aside at least two hours every evening to study. A mitigation action could be: putting the children to bed an hour earlier or enlisting the help of your spouse or nanny to manage bedtime routines.

In this section, also write out at least five tasks or actions that can help you achieve your goals. Assign a target date to each task, preferably on a weekly or monthly basis.

RELEVANT/REALISTIC

When your values are clear to you, making decisions becomes easier.

Every goal should be assessed to ensure it is worthwhile. Things to consider are: Does it matter to you? Is it reasonable and realistic and does it align with your overall goals and values? A relevant goal will usually answer questions such as:

- What is the objective behind the goal?
- Does this goal seem worthwhile?
- Does this goal align with my personal values? Is this the right time?
- Is it applicable based on my current circumstances and commitments?

Example

You might want to gain the skills to become a Project Manager within your current organization or seek opportunities elsewhere. Ask yourself if it is the right time to undertake the required training given you have very young children and work full-time? Have you also considered your spouse's goals? If your spouse is a busy Sales Executive who travels abroad frequently, would completing the training in your free time be possible? It may mean extended child-care, as neither of you will be available to take care of your children in the evening. Would this go against your family values?

TIME BOUND/TIMELY

Every great achievement requires time.

Every goal should have a deadline to specify when milestones can be achieved. Set deadlines for yourself against each of your milestones but keep them realistic and flexible.

Using the above example, gaining the skills and experience to become a Project Manager may require additional training or experience. Be realistic. How long will it take to acquire these additional qualifications? Do you need to gain specific project experience to be eligible for certain exams or qualifications? It's important to give yourself a realistic time frame for accomplishing the smaller goals that are necessary to achieving your final objective.

Example

"*Within the next six months*, I want to acquire a PRINCE2 qualification to build my knowledge and enable me to become a Project Manager within my organization's CRM department or to seek suitable external opportunities so I can build upon and progress my career through managing a successful project team."

"**Within the next year**, I want to shadow a Project Manager to learn the skills needed to become a successful Project Manager."

I have created a simple, and easy-to-use SMART Goals setting template which can be found in the Appendix. You can use it throughout the year for small, medium, or even big-sized goals such as career, business, training, fitness, diet, finance, volunteering, etc.

How SMART Can Be Applied to Your Personal Life

New Job

Perhaps one of your goals is to get a new job. Your goal statement might look like this: I want to get a new job as HR executive so I can build and progress my career through managing an organization's recruitment, learning, development, and employee performance programs while improving my personal finances.

Your milestone steps to achieve this goal may include:

- Revising and tailoring your CV
- Searching online for job opportunities
- Updating your LinkedIn profile
- Calling or e-mailing your recruiter
- Attending relevant professional networking events

A SMART goal setting for 'Search Online for Job Opportunities' might be: Check online for job opportunities at least four times every week, persistently searching for at least one hour each time. I should also create job alerts on the job sites my desired job can be found.

Travel

Have you always dreamed of traveling the world, but it's never happened?

Maybe that's because you don't have the time, money, or adequate childcare; hence, you keep putting it off every year. Try setting SMART goals to help make your travel plans specific, measurable, achievable, relevant, and time bound. You might find the real reason you haven't traveled is because your plans have been unattainable or unfocused. Think about how you can adjust your vision and rephrase it as a SMART goal, so you can make your travel dreams come true.

Below is an example of what a travel goal could look like:

I intend to visit one country in Europe over a four-day period, so I can learn about a new culture. I will enlist the support of my husband (or mum, sister, mother-in-law, aunt, brother, etc.) to help with childcare; I will provide at least four months' notice to ensure they can plan for it. I will save £50 every month to go towards my travel fund. I will research budget travel deals and commit to spend a maximum of £350 on the trip.

Return to Work Goal Statement

I want to return to a challenging but flexible job for four days a week that offers me the ability to work from home at least once or twice a week. This will enable me do the school runs and spend more time with my children.

Communicate What is Important to You

A lot of people are afraid to say what they want. That is why they don't usually get what they want. —Madonna

Once you've identified what is important to you based on your values and goals, the next thing to do is to communicate them openly with your spouse, boss, and any other key figure in your life. Don't expect your boss to guess what makes you feel fulfilled. Do you need to undertake a new qualification to enable you change jobs? Do you want to work towards achieving a promotion? Do you want to leave work an hour early to attend a professional workshop? Do you need to leave work at 5pm so you can pick up your child from the nursery or have dinner with your family? Do you need your husband to leave work at 5pm twice a week to relieve the nanny? Do you need to be able to leave work at 12pm to attend a gym class? Once you define what it is you want, you need to be transparent about it to get the required support. Tell whoever your choices will affect or impact.

When you let people know how serious you are about succeeding in your career, you will be surprised by how much they are willing to help you. Tell your husband why it is important that you find a new job or get a promotion. Tell your boss why you think you deserve a promotion. Explain to your children why mummy cannot put them to bed every single night. Furthermore, make a conscious choice to continually talk about what is or isn't working and make decisions to change direction if needed. If you find that you are stuck with your job or your organisation does not support your career growth and progress then maybe it's time for a change. You're allowed to change your mind; you have choices. You're allowed to change career paths. You're permitted to change your dreams. Just don't get stuck.

Mummy, What Do You Do at Work?
My job is a lead business analyst within technology in the financial services industry which entails partnering with clients to deliver software solutions that provide value and meet business needs. One of my top priorities is to make sure my children understand what I do for a living. Even though my sons are only five and two years old, I try to make them appreciate and value the hard

work and effort I put in daily. If you have not done this before, I suggest you sit with your children and explain, in the simplest terms, what your job involves.

I was one of the volunteers at a local primary school for their careers day and we were split into small groups of ten. I had to explain my job to children aged six and seven. I described to them how I and my team build software, some of which are quite like the gaming apps they play with on their tablets, but mine help people make good decisions with their money. One of the children asked me if we play games on the computer at work. It sounded funny at the time, but the fact I shared my work with them made me realise that if you cannot explain what you do to a six-year-old, then maybe you don't really understand your work. Prominent jobs like doctors or architects will be easier to explain to children. Less obvious jobs will be more challenging to define but it is important to start the conversation.

I have brought my children to work a few times. They do attend my office day care occasionally. Initially, my older son thought we just had fabulous parties in the office, as his first memory of my office when he was three was at the office annual children Christmas party. My older son would say, *"Mummy, I love your office. It's so cool."* But now that he's five, he's beginning to understand that we do serious work in the office. I have shown him some of my spread sheets and reports. I can see that he tries to relate my work to his school setup hence it's not surprising when he asks "mummy, *who is your head teacher? Are they nice? Do they open the gate for you? Do you have class assembly?"* I will encourage you to bring home suitable objects from work whenever possible; annual reports, bank cards, a rubber glove (if you're a doctor or nurse), or a business card is certain to spark their curiosity. No matter what your job is, start talking to your children about your work.

> **MUMMY'S CORNER**
>
> **What is your current job? What has been one of your biggest career challenges and how did you overcome it?**
>
> I'm a medical doctor in the United Kingdom and leading in a male and Caucasian-dominated environment. I overcome my challenges by believing in myself.
> **Dr Monica, mum of three**
>
> I am a Business Analyst at an investment bank in the financial sector. It entails constant learning and challenging my clients to give them the best solution to their problems. Being 100% at work while juggling sleepless nights has been my biggest challenge. Having a job that is challenging and keeps me busy helps combat this. I love taking a walk to get some fresh air, taking a ten-minute break somewhere quiet or, if all else fails, standing while I work for an hour or so.
> **Melinda, mum of two**
>
> I am an accountant. I perform the analysis of financial information for finance and non-finance audiences. I also report on trends in business, variance analysis in financial reports, and production of management and financial accounts. I would say my biggest career challenge has been

transitioning from banking to a more commercial business. I started my career in banking and always hated it. I never liked the industry. I am a qualified accountant. However, I had to study accounting because my university didn't offer a degree in medicine at the time.

Abby, mum of one

I am a registered nurse and my job entails being the patient's advocate and lots of nursing interventions. In addition, it involves constant learning. You seriously can't get bored. The fact you are dealing with people's lives is already challenging. I mean, sometimes you get yelled at from either the patient or a family member. How do I overcome it? I don't take it personally; I just pray for them.

Melanie, mum of one

I currently work in the transport industry in Client Services. My biggest career challenge was when I changed my career from the fashion industry to corporate. I am very passionate about fashion and I love the industry. However, it is not a mummy-friendly career. I love spending time with my children, so it was a very smart move and I must say I love it.

Glory, mum of three

I work as a Senior Business Analyst in the Credit Risk Department at Deutsche Bank, Canary Wharf London. It is a project-based role and it requires delivering compulsory documentation and working within specified timelines. There are so many challenges I face daily, like tight delivery timelines, difficulties communicating with other teams or stakeholders, etc. I really need to manage my time wisely when I am at work and make sure I have my work done within the working hours.

Sunny, mum of two

I currently work in banking as a Project Manager delivering regulatory initiatives. Whilst I immensely enjoy working in banking, I have simultaneously been producing a talk show – Hewnlife Talks, an internet-based (YouTube) show that aims to put a spotlight on a wide range of subjects impacting a vast number of people within our communities.

Olamide, mum of two

I am a Kumon instructor. The tutoring programme has two key subjects: Maths and English. The biggest challenge is always childcare and having enough time for the children. That is why I went for something that is flexible with my time.

Omolade, mum of two

I just moved to a new job after maternity leave, but before I was a team leader and Senior Researcher for a policy think tank chaired by his Royal Highness Prince el Hassan. The biggest challenge was proving to my Foreign Director that Jordanians, and especially women, are qualified, educated, and know better than her in the local context. Hence, we are better at our jobs.

Lara, mum of two

I have recently joined the Compliance and AFC training team. I joined the team in January 2017. I am in charge of rolling out eLearning courses globally to employees. Since returning from maternity leave and starting a new role, it has been hard to become a first-time mum, learning to be a working mum, and learning a new role. When I left, I had ten years' experience and would have felt much more comfortable returning to what I know but I applied for flexible work and it was declined. I was then approached about a job share opportunity which was very appealing to me, as I was already nervous about coming back and leaving my daughter. Learning this new role whilst my brain was at home/everywhere else has been the toughest and biggest challenge so far.

Kelly, mum of one

I am a Programme Manager within Financial Services. I am responsible for delivery of different projects in my division, and with holding people to account on their committed deadlines and deliverables to make my project successful.

Elizabeth, mum of two

Reflection

1. Reassess and write down your why. What are you best at and really enjoy doing? Complete the Vision Board template in the appendix. Place it somewhere visible where you can see it every day.
2. Identify three top goals (e.g. career, parenting, fitness) you would like to achieve within the next three to six months. Use the Goal setting template in the appendix as a guide.
3. Explain your job to your child.

Chapter Two: From Working Lady to Working Mum

When new mums come back to work after a maternity leave they need someone to tell them, "You are likely to feel overwhelmed and anxious. It is okay to feel overwhelmed and anxious. You won't always feel overwhelmed and anxious."

Anne-Marie Slaughter's book *Unfinished Business: Women, Men, Work, and Family* made me feel relieved to be working in the United Kingdom where paid maternity leave and protected rights for part-time mums and pregnant workers is the norm. This isn't always the case in other countries, unfortunately. This meant that when I celebrated a full year of returning to work after having my second son, I was rarely using words like dread, frustration, suffering, survival, etc. to describe my working life. Regardless, the transition from being a working girl to being at home with a baby can be daunting, if not properly planned and managed. Based on the sharing of experiences, advice, and tips of other working mums, I have formulated a maternity leave checklist which covers the important detail you will need.

Familiarise Yourself with the Relevant Laws

In the UK, employees have a right to take up to a year of maternity leave. It doesn't matter how long you've worked for your employer, how much you are paid, or how many hours a week you work. Regardless of where you're based, ensure you know your rights around leave, pay, and discrimination because you never know when you might have to fight for them. Get a copy of your company's employee handbook to learn about your company's policies on maternity leave. Find out if there are exceptions or unwritten rules. Ask your company's HR advisor to guide you in the process. If, like many women, you're not comfortable telling anyone about your pregnancy until your first trimester is over, just reading the information is a helpful start.

Informing Your Boss

While you're understandably distracted by the excitement and nerves that come with bringing a new life into the world, controlling your message is very important. Privacy is quite elusive these days. Whether knowingly or unknowingly, many of us are connected to our colleagues and bosses on social media platforms; we live in a digital world where secrets are hard to keep. You wouldn't want to be like the woman who phoned in sick and then posted Instagram photos of herself on the beach with a cocktail in hand!

Top Tip: Please don't post a photo of your positive pregnancy test on social media straight away.

Most women tell their employer they're pregnant around the end of the first trimester or early into their second trimester. That's partially because by that time risk of miscarriage is significantly reduced. However, sometimes early pregnancy symptoms, such as severe morning sickness, may leave you with less flexibility and choice about when to share the news. You should tell your manager the news face-to-face if possible.

Don't Leave Until You Leave

In her book *Lean In: Women, Work, and the Will to Lead*, Sheryl Sandberg recognised that many young women lean back earlier than required. I think what Sheryl meant by *'don't leave before you leave'*" is that women who plan to become mums in the foreseeable or distant future should not just be content with their jobs because they are planning on maternity leave. This means women should strive to get a challenging, fulfilling, and enjoyable job before they take maternity leave because that fantastic job might be the motivation to make them return to work after the baby's born.

Top Tip: For ambitious women who desire great careers or have set high career goals for themselves and want to have children, being in a great job could be motivation to return to work and succeed in reaching career goals.

For this group of women, the ideal time to scale down or take a step back is when a break is needed or just before a child arrives, not before and certainly not years in advance. It is in fact the critical time to lean in and apply for a new position, assuming an opportunity presents itself or self-promoting the great work and contributions you have already delivered is appropriate. This is not the time to check out of your career if you aspire to get to a leadership position. I wish someone had told me this because I would have put my hand up a bit more, even after finding out I was pregnant.

On the other hand, assuming you are in a job that you don't enjoy, you really should try to 'leave before you leave' by finding something new internally or externally. In this case, the first step would be to find a job worth leaning into and coming back to. Based on my own experiences, the 'leaning in' should come naturally and easily.

During Your Last Trimester

During your last trimester, you should create a written maternity leave plan that you are comfortable handing over and leaving with your manager. This is a large project and should cover what communication (if any) you plan on keeping with the office while you're out and whether you would have a replacement in place before you leave.

Create a physical and online folder for all your maternity leave-related documents. In this folder, you can put all HR forms, Maternity certificates, insurance documentation, benefits information, e-mails from HR or your manager pertaining to your leave, and all other related information. Make copies of any paperwork you fill out and submit. These copies can be kept in your folder too.

Start talking to colleagues in your department about their maternity leave experiences. Invite them to have a coffee or lunch with you and ask for tips and advice about how to manage your maternity leave and the subsequent return to work.

Preparing for Baby's Arrival

I worked all the way up to three weeks before the due date of my first baby's birth. This meant I still had time for last minute preparations. If you feel as though you're not organised before your baby's arrival, write a list of what needs to be done. Then prioritise everything. There will probably be items which can wait until after the baby is born. I went through an intensive nesting phase for my first baby, which involved me getting my husband to decorate the baby room and setting everything in place; the cot, the dresser, and everything else had to be properly arranged. I travelled to the United States at the start of my third trimester to shop for baby clothes that he eventually outgrew too quickly.

Now I regret going so overboard and putting myself through such stress by ensuring I ticked off every single item on my list and buying everything in advance. My learnings from that experience gave me insight, and for my second baby I became pretty laid back. I had same-sex babies and could, therefore, re-use most of the items.

What to Put on Your Priority List

- Somewhere for baby to sleep: Moses basket, crib, baby blankets, sheets
- Bottles, sterilising unit (even if you plan to breast feed, you may need emergency backup)
- Your hospital bag with nightdress, nursing bras, maternity pads, comfortable knickers, toiletries

- Baby's hospital bag with first-size sleep suits, nappies, cotton wool, hat, going-home outfit
- Pram, car seat, basics such as baby bath, towels, creams

Remember, anything else can be bought after baby is born, or you can ask family, friends, or neighbours to help attain necessities. Amazon, Mothercare, and Kiddicare usually offer next day or even same-day delivery for many items, so don't worry. Housework and decorating can also wait. The baby can easily sleep in your room for the first three to nine months, so even the decoration of the nursery can be put on hold if you find you're getting overwhelmed.

Get Fit

I used to be size eight pre-baby and shifted slightly towards a size ten post-baby number two but, overall, I managed to maintain my figure despite two pregnancies. I still get asked how I have been able to maintain my body weight and my honest answer is 'I exercised'. I was super active and ate healthy foods throughout my pregnancies. Exercise during pregnancy has tremendous benefits for the mum-to-be; it can result in shorter times in labour, easier births, and faster returns to pre-pregnancy figures. Being pregnant doesn't mean you have to stop exercising. By maintaining a regular exercise routine and eating a wide variety of wholesome foods, you can conserve your fitness and health during this time. If possible, find an antenatal fitness group in your area. Always follow your doctor's advice. Don't overdo it. Choose low-impact, low-risk exercises such as walking, swimming, yoga and dance that work for your body. I attended several antenatal yoga sessions that were offered by my office gym and I met and bonded with other mums while I was there. Those friendships made at the antenatal classes continue to this day.

Allow Yourself Some 'Me' Time

Try to give yourself some down time between leaving work and the baby's arrival. Ideally, when all your shopping and preparations for your baby are finished, try to concentrate on relaxing activities such as sleeping, reading, and watching your favourite television show, simple pleasures that are soon to become precious luxuries. Check that you have packed your hospital bag.

How to Cope with Baby Blues and Mild Post-Natal Depression

Welcoming a new baby into your life is one of the most intense experiences women go through. Having a baby can be stressful no matter how long you've waited for it or how much you have prepared for it. Considering sleep deprivation, new responsibilities, and lack of time, it's no surprise a lot of new mums feel they're on an emotional rollercoaster. After I had my first baby, I really struggled with anxiety, sadness, weight reduction, and loss of appetite. I think what triggered it was the fact I had an emergency C-section after such a 'perfect' pregnancy and it just made everything worse afterwards. It all started with the pain and then I felt guilty about not being able to give my new-born baby my "all". What made me feel terrible was that even after six weeks of post-partum, I still felt so much pain. Although I was not officially diagnosed, my early symptoms clearly suggested mild post-natal depression, or as it is also known: the baby blues. I felt tearful, overwhelmed, and emotionally fragile. Although the baby was doing well, I was really struggling with breastfeeding—he with latching on and me with being able to connect with him properly. This was a far cry from my second baby, which was a natural birth. If anyone is still wondering whether vaginal birth after C-section is possible, I'll tell you it certainly is. Although I had an acute chest infection around my due date (which led me to be in hospital admission three days before my due date), I didn't feel as overwhelmed or anxious as I had with my first baby.

Baby blues are perfectly normal. Generally, they start within the first couple of days after delivery and may last for up to two weeks postpartum but, if your symptoms don't go away after a few weeks or if they get worse, you may be suffering from postpartum depression. According to the National Health Service, one in every ten women struggle from postpartum depression. I feel safe in saying that many of the root causes, at least in my case, were not just lack of support, but a lack of required backing and not being confident enough to ask for the right level of help and care.

I was very blessed to have both my mum and mother-in-law living with us and helping with my first baby. They were present at the hospital when my first son was born. My mum, who is a government official in Nigeria, took time off work to visit and stay with us for six weeks. Her support in our new journey was invaluable. Similarly, my mother-in-law came to stay for three months to help with the baby. Two months after my first son was born, my mum returned to Nigeria and I was left at home with my mother-in-law. One morning, I was hungry but couldn't use the kitchen because my mother-in-law seemed very busy in that area; what's more, I didn't want to face her because I hadn't showered and wasn't wearing a bra. I also had a headache and didn't feel very chatty. I didn't want to interrupt her to ask if she could help me by watching over the baby. That meant I couldn't shower because I didn't know what to do with the baby while in the shower. *What if he cries? What will my mother-in-law think?* I was afraid she'd think I could not take care of my own child. But I was hungry and wanted tea and toast. So, I sat in my room and cried whilst breastfeeding my baby. I was in my pyjamas, famished and feeling dreadful until my mother-in-law finally came upstairs to check on me. She could tell I was struggling, so she took the baby and said she had prepared brunch —a rice dish. She invited me to go downstairs to help myself to the food but when I smelled the food I completely lost my appetite and opted to take a shower instead.

I was also extremely overwhelmed and vulnerable and I think many new mums can relate to this. I didn't know how to ask for help and the help I was being offered wasn't what I wanted or needed. Whilst my mother-in-law was being helpful by organizing food, I didn't have the appetite to eat the types of food she was preparing. When vulnerable and emotional, a simple slice of toast and some hot sweet tea would have been perfect, but I didn't even know how to ask for that. Such a simple task seemed to be so daunting.

On top of feeling vulnerable, I didn't have the energy to socialise anymore. I used to love hanging out with my friends. Having the baby changed all that and those 'loss' emotions began to pile on the feelings of sadness.

I read stories of many mums fearing being judged, unnecessarily hospitalised, or visited by Social Services. Some women had these things happen to them after reaching out for help, which is probably why many women never get diagnosed. Thus, I have written down some handy tips to help cope with post baby blues at home and in everyday life.

Talk About Your Feelings

Communicate with those around you. Talk to your husband, friends, family, and other mums. Explain how you are feeling and ask for support. Speak to your health visitor about what you're going through. Being open and sharing your concerns will help you and others understand and overcome these problems. If you're struggling with postnatal depression, it's okay to ask your doctor for help. If you're ashamed to speak to your family, there are many online forums, such as Netmums, that support mothers and parents. Talking openly to other mums can relieve the burden and sense of isolation. It doesn't matter who you talk to as long as that person is willing to listen without judgment and offer reassurance and support.

Take Time for Yourself and Ask for Help
Set some quality time aside for you to relax and take a little break from your mum duties. Find small ways to pamper yourself, like taking a bubble bath, enjoying a hot cup of tea, burning light scented candles, or getting a massage. You may find it helpful to fit some dedicated 'me time' into your weekly schedule. I wish I had done this after having my first baby. Self-care is not vanity; you need to take your physical and mental health seriously and support yourself with a healthy diet, plenty of rest, and some fun too. Get into the habit of eating nutritious foods to help you feel better and give your body the nutrients it needs.

Ask your husband or another trusted adult to look after the baby for an hour or two so you can go for a walk, take a nap, go to a movie, or do some yoga and meditation. Even if you can only get out of the house between breastfeeding sessions for a few minutes, you can use that time to go on a short walk.

Nurture the Relationship with Your Husband
Many things change after the birth of a baby, including roles and expectations. For many couples, a key source of strain and stress is the post-baby division of

the household and childcare responsibilities. Instead of finger-pointing, remember that you're in this together. If you tackle parenting challenges as a team, you'll become an even stronger unit. It's important to talk about your issues rather than letting them build up. Don't assume your husband knows how you feel or knows what you need.

It's essential to make time for just the two of you so that you can reconnect and bond. You don't need to go out on a date to enjoy each other's company. Even spending thirty minutes together on the sofa over a cup of tea when the baby is asleep can make a big difference in your feelings of closeness and intimacy.

Keep a Gratitude Journal

Rather than focusing on the negatives, go for the positive by keeping a gratitude journal. Count your blessings and think about all the things that have gone well. Write them down and be grateful for them. I enjoyed many aspects of my postpartum journey. My mum and mother-in-law spoiled me with breakfasts in bed and helped with bathing and looking after the baby. We received several bouquets from colleagues and friends after our son was born and he too received so many gifts. My pastor's wife came bearing beautiful gifts for not only the baby but also for me. I really loved it.

Take each day as it happens and look for one thing that is good each day. It could be that you managed a hot meal before noon, or that your baby finally had a dirty nappy, or you did the laundry. Whatever it is, there will be something good that happened that day. You will soon find yourself focusing on positive moments rather than the negatives. As I expressed my gratitude for the things I hadn't previously paid attention to, like the gift of motherhood, my home, my health, a good meal, and good music, I began to be more mindfully aware throughout the day. This was one of the reasons I started actively blogging—it was an outlet to express myself. This helped a lot during my second postpartum journey.

Don't Try to Be Perfect

Cut yourself some slack. Don't be so hard on yourself. Don't try to do everything yourself. It's so tempting to feel guilty and responsible for getting the entire household chores done on top of caring for a tiny new-born, but don't think it's what you must do. Nurturing a new-born is a full-time job. Enjoy the journey as much as possible.

Develop a Support Network

As someone with very little close local support, after my mums went back to Nigeria I found my new mum friends a lifeline. They helped me vent all my feelings and see things in perspective. If you don't have any friends, use a mummy friendship app or attend a local mum class where you can make new like-minded mum friends.

One of the things I found difficult as a new mum was feeling completely alone breastfeeding at 2am. Having people you can communicate with that are going through similar situations is a life saver, even if it is mums who live a thousand miles away.

It is important to book an appointment with your doctor if you experience feelings of depression after birth, especially if after a couple weeks the sensations get worse and continue over time. Your doctor can point you in the right direction to get the support you need. Apart from family and close friends, there are other places you can reach out to for support:

- Speak to your midwife or health visitor.
- Speak to another mum from work.
- Contact your pastor's wife or another leader in your faith community.
- Ask around about any local support groups for breastfeeding or PND.
- Chat online with other mums in forums like *Baby Centre*.

Note: If you're having suicidal thoughts or thoughts about harming yourself or baby, call your local emergency services immediately.

I asked five mothers their top tip on how a new mum can deal with baby blues and mild PND. Here are their responses:

- *Speaking from experience. Get out. Go meet people. It's really tough and staying cooped up inside won't help. You will most likely meet someone who is going through the exact same thing you are.*
- *Get out of the house. As daunting as it seems you will be glad you did. I would sometimes just put baby in the pram and walk. It's refreshing and makes you feel amazing. Even a little walk to the local shop will do you the world of good, trust me mama.*
- *Ask for help. I felt like I had to have my baby at all times in order to be a good mother and that having even a small break was bad and wrong and that made my symptoms even worse. Sometimes you just need a little breather to remind yourself that you are doing okay. Know that you're not alone, PND can strike anyone, from any background, with any life, so many more people battle it than you ever realise. Just reach out. Also, there are so many charities out there that offer support that you can contact with a phone call or even an email.*

- *Don't try to do everything! It's so tempting to feel guilty and responsible for getting all the household work done on top of caring for a tiny newborn, but don't think it's what you have to do.*
- *Make new mummy friends. If you can't find any local, get onto a mummy friendship app such as Mush or take a class or two. Take each day as it happens and look for one thing that's good each day. It could be you and your baby got dressed before twelve.*

During Your Maternity Leave

Whilst I was at home on maternity leave, my husband would return from work in the evening to find me still in my pyjamas with my hair uncombed and in pretty much the same state he had left me in. He would ask, "What have you been doing all day?" I would then go on to narrate all the mummy duties which ranged from bathing baby, breastfeeding, laundry, nappy changing, pacifying crying baby, cleaning, ironing, etc. Those few days I couldn't manage time for a shower were because I was overwhelmed with the tasks before me. They prevented me from doing anything else outside of minding the baby. I'm sure other mums can relate to this. Of course, with time I got more organized—mainly from receiving good advice and ideas from other experienced mums on what worked for them. One revelation came when I got a very good bouncer that seemed to entertain my baby for longer periods of time, which meant I could have a shower and eat my meals in peace. I found co-sleeping to be very hard too, as I barely got any sleep, so I researched the topic and finally found a systemic approach to sleep train my baby at eight months. It was a tough process, but it led me to determine a more sustainable approach that worked well and made my life a little bit easier. It is important to get into a routine as soon as possible so you can truly enjoy being a mum.

Making the Most of Your Maternity Leave

There's more to maternity leave than breastfeeding, changing nappies, and watching Jeremy Kyle or Loose Women. Remember to make it a precious and special time for you and your baby. Soon enough it will become just a memory, so create opportunities and ways to make your maternity leave enjoyable and productive for both you and your little one.

Accept that the First Weeks Will Be Hard

The first few weeks with a new-born are a shock to everyone's system. You are getting used to being a sleep-deprived, milk-leaking mum, your baby is adjusting to living outside the comfort of your warm womb, and your husband is adjusting to being a dad.

This is not the time to pressure yourself into running around being social or productive. Simply taking a short walk or a shower can feel like a major accomplishment. That's not to say you shouldn't make plans, just make sure the plans are on your terms and work for you.

Learn to Live in the Moment

When you bring your attention to what is happening right now, there is no room for worrying about the future or dwelling on the past. There is only what is going on in the moment, and this likely means you are taking care of your new-born. That is where your attention is.

Do you get sad about heading back to work? If so, it's super important to live in the moment while you're on maternity leave. Yes, when you head back to work it's going to be tough, but you are not going back to work until your maternity leave is over—which means not today.

Instead of letting your emotions run wild, bring your attention to the present moment. Practicing how thankful you are will bring you joy and will hopefully stop any tears from pouring out. Spend the day in your sleep wear. Why? Because:

- you can.
- you deserve it.

Explore Your Neighbourhood

It is important to get dressed and out of the house, ideally once every other day, for your own sanity and the sake of your baby. Remember, babies need fresh air. My health visitor provided me with a list of several baby and breastfeeding groups where I could meet with other mums and chat with health visitors about any concerns I may have had. Be sure to talk to your midwife or health visitor and get points of contact for these support groups. Ensure you check out your nearest local community or council-funded children's centre.

For activities that must be block booked as a course, ask if you can do a trial session before committing. Baby classes in the UK can cost from around £4 per session, but some activities and play groups are free.

When I was on maternity leave, I attended baby sensory, baby massage, music, and singing groups and even swimming classes. Some groups, such as the breastfeeding support, were free but others, like baby sensory, charge every term or have a 'drop-in' entrance fee. The baby sensory group was very popular and had a waiting list. You could even choose to set up your own group with a few local mums. Invite them round for tea and then change locations each week to someone else's house or baby-friendly coffee shop.

Many cinemas run special baby cinema screenings for new mums and babies. You might not catch much of the film, but you can take a couple of hours out, have some popcorn, and breastfeed in public without fear of being judged.

Working mums can really benefit from friendships with other working mums because they often have the same schedules and experience similar issues. It is very important to start building your mum support system early on. I wish someone had told me how important this is. All these contacts will come in handy when you have to return to work. Trust me, you will need quick information about something baby-related or need someone to help pick up your child when you get stuck in traffic. Besides, it's good for your baby to learn to socialise early on, to become flexible, and get used to other people, babies, and locations.

New Mum Self-Care Tips

- Take turns with your husband; share the responsibility of getting up with the baby at night.
- If possible, sleep when the baby is sleeping.
- Have a long bubble bath.
- Take a ten-minute walk.
- Schedule a hair or nail appointment.
- Read a book.
- Join a local mum and baby group.
- Don't lose yourself. Enjoy the motherhood transition.

- You can't do it all. Take a break
- Take time and discover your inner strength.
- Children are different, so know what works best for yours.
- Delegate, accept help, and trust your spouse when he says he can sort things out.

Enjoy Your Time off Work

My first maternity leave was exhausting because I had no clue what I was doing until around eight months and by then my maternity leave was almost over. However, a good portion of my leave was filled with sleep-ins, cuddles, and lunch dates with friends who had just become mums as well. I miss those times and feel I won't get that again now that I have a second baby and have returned to work.

It didn't feel like a vacation where you get to go on tours, shopping, or try out new food. You might not get much time to watch Netflix because you end up falling asleep half way through every episode or get interrupted and have to re-watch the same episode three times.

Apart from the breastfeeding and baby groups, which I totally enjoyed, the most memorable times during my first maternity leave was our travels. During my maternity leave, we visited Algarve and California. Portugal was the first country we took my older son to when he was a little more than five months old. It's proved to be very memorable for us because he grew out his first two teeth whilst there. We went during the month of September; hence, the weather was nice with the sea still very warm but not too hot. One thing I noted was how child-friendly it was; we saw children everywhere—in strollers, on foot, in restaurants, even in bars, and it was obvious the Portuguese are very accommodating towards children.

Having said this, don't head into the big wide world until you are ready. Make sure those first couple of weeks or months are spent on the sofa eating, drinking, and feeding the baby as much as possible. Most of all, just enjoy your time together, as the end of maternity leave comes around way too quickly.

Keeping in Touch with Work

When you are no longer 'part' of a company, its values, or its routines, you can feel disconnected and that the only option is all or nothing. Yet the area in between, particularly for parents focusing on caring for their children, can be hugely liberating and have lifelong benefits for your career and your family.

In the UK, entitled employees can work up to ten days during their maternity leave. These days are called 'keeping-in-touch' days. Keeping-in-touch days are optional and both employee and employer need to agree on them. Keeping-in-touch days are intended to help you stay 'synced' with your workplace and take on a few hours of work without affecting your statutory pay. These days help you ease into your eventual return to work. You're entitled to keeping-in-touch days if you are eligible for statutory maternity pay, regardless of the hours you work. For my second baby, I used five of my keeping-in-touch days to bring my baby in to meet my team, for my performance review, and to catch up with my line manager over the phone. Re-skill yourself in the place and time available to you. Read professional books. Take online courses. Update your LinkedIn profile regularly and share your views and topics on relevant topics. If you feel passionate about blogging, write and share your views, findings, and experiences.

Preparing for Your Return

After I returned to work from being on my second maternity leave, I found I was not just grateful to have had the opportunity to go to work, continue my career, and have those rare moments when I'm able to drink tea whilst it's still hot, but I also appreciated the fact my employer supports flexible and part-time working. My employer also has a hot desking policy, which means I can work remotely from home once or twice every week without having to fight for it. Hot desking is a flexible work space sharing model in which employees outnumber desks, thus it involves allocating desks to employees when they are required or on a Rota system rather than giving each staff member a permanent desk. Additionally, it comprises multiple staff using a single physical work station during different time periods. It is becoming a common practice for big organizations located in high demand and expensive locations, such as Canary Wharf and the City of London. This is done to save on building and infrastructure costs.

The transition period from working lady to working mum is a big deal and there are many changes to manage. I did some research and opted to use a trusted and referred weekday nanny. This was the easiest option for me because I had a daily 75-minute each way commute to work. My nanny started her duties a few weeks before my work recommencement date, which meant I was able to spend some quality time with her and give full practical knowledge of my child's routine.

We agreed her working hours were to be 7am-6:30pm, which meant I wouldn't have to rise earlier in the morning to get baby ready. When he was eighteen months old, he started attending day care and on those mornings I or my husband had to drop him off on our way to work.

Find a Suitable Childcare Option

From day care centres, nannies, au pairs, and childminders to play groups and after-school clubs, there is a large range of childcare services available in most countries, provided both within the home and outside of it. Each service is slightly different and has different benefits and associated costs. The cost and availability of suitable childcare is the biggest problem most working mums in the United Kingdom face. The cost of childcare had risen to seven times faster than wages since 2008. According to a 2017 research by the family and childcare trust, the average cost of sending a child under two to a full-time nursery in London is around £232 per week. Currently, the full-time children's day care costs for my toddler are around £1100 per month. I have always treated childcare costs like a mortgage because you still have to pay during holidays and when your child is off sick. This means those who aren't in highly-paid jobs or who don't have a husband or grandparents to help look after the children, re-entering the work place can be close to impossible. If you establish that your childcare costs are around £1100 per month and you are earning circa £1700 per month after tax (like one of the mums from my community), then you must evaluate whether working in that job is worth it. Maybe a career change or starting a new business should be your next goal.

Finding good, quality childcare is a big challenge for working mums. Hence, it's very important to do your research in advance.

The health visitor directed me to my local council who provided an up-to-date list of approved childcare centres in my area. The list they gave included child-minders, day care nurseries, babysitters, and nannies. In the five years since becoming a mum, I have used a combination of nanny and day care centres, so I am, therefore, able to provide tips on these two options. If you choose to wait until the child is born to think about childcare, it can be useful. It will give you time to think carefully about what type of childcare is likely to suit your child based on his habits and behaviours. Is he/she outgoing and receptive to new people and environments? Then a larger, busier nursery will suit him/her. Or would he/she feel more secure in a small, home-based setting with a child-minder? Before you start your research, bear in mind the following:

- You must do what works for your family based on your circumstances. There is no one-size fits all solution.
- The quality of care you choose is more important than the form it takes. A good nanny, an outstanding nursery, a good child-minder, or even a hands-on and competent grandparent could work just fine.
- To make it easier to find good childcare, you need to have a clear idea of what hours and pattern of care you require based on your and your spouse's working hours.
- Using more than one childcare provider could open further opportunities for your child to experience alternative play, learning, and interactions in different settings.

Advice on Day Care Centres

Most good full-day care centres have a long waiting list, so try to get on the list in advance—ideally during your pregnancy. My first born was unable to start day care until he was eighteen months old, and this was due to the waiting list at my preferred centre.

Here are some top tips to finding suitable day care:

- Draw up a shortlist of childcare providers in your area using information from your local Family Information Service or online research. Google will become your best friend!
- Phone your shortlist to check their working hours, weekly costs, and availability.
- Visit your top providers, ideally with your husband or mum to ensure 'four-eye check'.
- Ask as many questions as possible. I approached each with a long list of questions such as: What is the ratio of staff to children? What activities are planned each day? Is the food prepared on site?
- Check their quality standards and inspection information from the relevant body that regulates early year education.
- Get feedback from other mums and neighbours; use their experiences as a source of reference.
- Reserve a place in your chosen setting.
- Have backup care in place e.g. a child-minder, nanny, babysitter, or neighbour.

Advice on Hiring a Nanny

I wanted to go out and change the world, but I couldn't find a suitable nanny.

I was very fortunate to have had an amazing nanny for more than three years. She had been with us since my first born was a year old. Unfortunately, she chose to leave to pursue other career opportunities and I had to start again. The search for a nanny can be daunting and the thought of leaving your newborn or toddler with a stranger can be overwhelming. It doesn't have to be. My old nanny was highly recommended by one of my uncles, which eased the burden of searching for a suitable candidate. While many reputable agencies are willing to help you find applicants, you can also recruit, interview, and hire nannies on your own.

Here are some tips that can help in this process:

- Seek referrals when hiring nannies. Tell everybody you know that you are looking for a nanny. The best way to find someone is through word of mouth. Advertise on Gumtree and your local mum Facebook groups stating your requirements.
- Failing referral, make sure to use a reputable nanny agency. *Care.com* and *Childcare.com* are very popular search sites in the UK.
- Before you even start the interview process, develop a written description of your nanny position. Is it a live-in position? What are the working hours? What are the responsibilities? Is it childcare? House maintenance? Activities management? Tutoring or education-focused?
- Each candidate should be interviewed face-to-face or via Skype, if based outside your locality.
- Check references and run background checks before hiring.
- Agree on a clear list of responsibilities and expectations. This has to be a win-win for both parties; be sure to set boundaries.
- Offer your candidates a trial run whilst you are present.

- Make sure the candidate has previous childcare experience; you don't want them learning on your child.
- Never rely on a nanny to do everything; always check in to be sure things are going as expected.
- Show gratitude and reward them for their good work. Go the extra mile; perhaps buy them an unexpected gift. Give them a small tip or pay rise. Take them out to lunch. Remember their birthdays and special occasions. A happy employee will stay with you.
- Be patient, give them room for improvement, and acknowledge their efforts. Don't try to micro-manage them!
- Always have a backup plan e.g. a nursery, child-minder, mum friend, or neighbour.
- You might want to pay a little more than market rate so as not to risk losing your nanny to someone else who is paying more.
- Create a list of instructions the nanny can refer to when you are at work. This should include meal plans, allergies, medications, routines and schedules, and emergency contact numbers.

MUMMY'S CORNER

What is your top tip for childcare arrangements?

My top tip is to pay for good quality childcare and teach your children to be independent early.

Dr Monica, mum of three

Get childcare arrangements which will not bring additional stress to morning or evening travelling (especially if both parents need to commute). Also check various childcare scenarios to see which is most affordable while providing the required flexibility.

Melinda, mum of two

Be confident. Make sure you have arranged reliable childcare for your kid. I am very lucky to have a live-in nanny now. She has relieved of a lot of stress. I don't need to worry about train delays or housework. My suggestion is, use as much available help as possible to release your stress (grandparents, nannies, babysitters, cleaners etc.).

Sunny, mum of two

Use a registered nanny or nursery if you can afford it. Better still, get a trusted relative from your home country.

Abby, mum of one

Do your research and get to know a little bit about day care options. Not all day care facilities are good. Also, let your child start day care at least one or two weeks before returning to work in order to make the transition easier. It's not an easy time for parents and children and this window of opportunity will give the whole family time to adjust and adapt. In my case, my son started day care a month before I returned to work because in Canada we get one-year maternity leave. (Oh, how much I love Canada.) The first couple of days were rough but, after one week, he was smiling and happy.

Melanie, mum of one

Be as thorough as possible throughout your search, don't feel like you're being too picky, and listen to your gut instincts. It helps if you can find a provider who shares some of your values and you can bond with as it makes the whole experience more streamlined and rewarding.

Ifeyinwa, mum of five

If you can get your folks to help from overseas, it is a massive bonus. If not, try to work around your children's schedule so you don't lose out too much.

Omolade, mum of two

Don't be afraid to try something and change your mind. I changed my mind about a nursery I had chosen during settling in.

Elizabeth, mum of two

I live in a very small place where everyone knows everyone; this helped me in finding a good child-minder from recommendation. I made sure to choose a child-minder that I clicked with the second I met and who my daughter seemed to interact well with at the first meet. It took four months for my daughter to go to the child-minder without screaming. I remember getting to the train station, having cried the whole journey. But I decided to stick with it, as the child-minder reassured me five minutes after I left she was running around playing and now she waves me off. I also have an app with her updates and pictures and this really helps, as at the end of day you can read up on their day.

Kelly, mum of one

Establish Sane Working Schedule

During your final keeping-in-touch days, agree with your manager on your working hours and let them know if you will require flexible working arrangements. It's important to be upfront about any changes you may want. Most UK employers are obligated to consider flexible working requests and can only refuse if there are good and recognised business grounds for not being able to accommodate you. For example, if it is not possible to properly do your job in fewer days or hours. To request flexible working hours, most employers expect you to meet some criteria such as having continuously worked for the employers for twenty-six weeks prior to applying for changes.

An annual survey conducted by *working mother* in 2016 showed that 18% of mums (one in five) have been forced to leave their work when flexible working was disallowed. Adapting to work was tough when I had my first son, not just for me but for my family as well. Even though I could work part-time, there wasn't a hot desking' policy and working from home was at my boss's discretion on an ad hoc basis. After my second child's birth, I returned to work on a four-day basis and managed to get Mondays off to spend at home with my boys. On top of that, I am also able to work from home at least one day a week. Flexible and part-time working made it easier. That is probably the resounding reason why I still hold my current job. Here are some tips for requesting flexible working hours:

- Flexible working hours can usually be a negotiation process.
- Emphasise your continued commitment to the organisation and suggest ways in which you may be able to provide additional working hours in emergencies.
- Suggest who may be able to cover your work when you aren't there.

- Articulate how the work could be managed around your changing hours.
- Be prepared to be flexible too. Should your request be refused, they might be able to offer an alternative position within the company.

Split Shift

Building a successful career often requires more than forty hours a week, but you want to have a full family life as well. To strike this delicate balance, focus on arranging working hours whilst the children are in childcare and possibly put in some extra hours in the evening; these are key attainments for many women. It's about ensuring you make perfect use of all hours in the week, allowing you to make enough time for work but also plenty of time for your family. I once worked on a project with some Australian stakeholders which meant I had to log in regularly around 8pm to work with the operations team. This worked quite well because I could log out of work at 4pm and fulfil my mummy responsibilities and then log back in at 8pm to catch up with my Australian stakeholders. Nowadays, many organizations in the western world and emerging economies can accommodate a split shift for working mums or carers.

Working a split shift can be inconvenient because you can't concentrate your full work day into a single block of time. It is easier, however, than trying to combine part-time jobs into full-time hours and coordinating two or more differing employers. A split shift can be family-friendly, depending on your schedule. You can use the time between shifts to do school runs, care for your children, take them to appointments, or run other errands for friends or relatives.

Night work and unusually long hours can cause fatigue and sleep disruption/deprivation. If you can find a job or role that permits split shifts, it could be the ideal situation to support juggling work and family effectively.

After Your Return to Work

Consolidate Work and Home Calendars

When something unexpected turns up, have a calendar which shows both your personal and professional commitments, as well as your significant other's. While you're busy accommodating and getting your sick child to the doctor, you will want to know which meetings need cancelling or when you have to get coverage from your husband or backup caregiver because you can't miss work.

Go to Bed Early

Your first week back at work will probably be draining—no matter how prepared you are. So, if possible, try to go to bed early each evening. Sleep with earplugs and ask your husband to handle your child's 'night waking'. It may be energizing to be back at work, but you will need decent sleep to be productive.

Prioritise Unapologetically

Working mums aim to be brutally efficient; we have to be! You should identify key tasks that must be completed to get you up to speed at work. Everything else you'll get around to in time.

Tackle the most important things early in your work day; that will leave fewer loose ends if you get called to pick up a sick child from the nursery. Brace yourself; the first few months of group childcare are usually punctuated by colds, fevers, ear infections, and even chicken pox. The silver lining is that minor illnesses can strengthen your child's immune system.

Plan for Emergencies

I know you can't always plan for everything, but you can keep life's inevitable challenges from escalating into an emergency. Children will get sick. They will have doctor's appointments, half-days at school, sick days, snow days, holidays, half-terms, and school breaks. You and your spouse should have a plan for who will take time off work in these different scenarios. You might also want to enlist the help of other friends, family, or neighbours.

Ask ahead of time if they will be your back up care or if they will be able to pick your child up in an emergency. You'll feel a lot less stressed if you have a plan in place.

Give Yourself a Reward for a Job Well Done

After all this planning and transition, you deserve a treat. Propose a reward that will help you get through your first week back at work. Maybe it's a pedicure appointment or lunch date with one of your friends or even a Saturday morning snuggles in bed with your baby to reconnect after being apart all week. You deserve it and it will help refresh you for the second week back at work. You'll never know for sure how you'll feel during your motherhood transitional challenge, but don't make any hasty decisions about your future based on the first week. Instead, notice how you feel and what you like or dislike about it. If uneasy feelings persist after a few weeks or months, you may want to change your work pattern or childcare situation.

Now You are Back to Work

Having suitable childcare and a backup plan in place will make the transition back to work easier. When I returned to work the second time, I went back on a four-day week basis whilst still having a weekday nanny. My husband also had flexible working arrangements and was able to work from home two days a week. I can work from home two days a week depending on my work schedule, so our time is becoming more suited to our combined lifestyles.

I still had anxiety going back to work and had many questions flooding my thoughts. How would my four-year-old son cope in my absence, as he seems to have gotten used to me being at home with him? How would my ten-month-old son adjust to not seeing me as often? How would I cope with my work load? How would I juggle everything?

The first few weeks weren't as easy as I thought. I dived head first into the pressurised work environment and struggled with feelings of guilt about going back. I had anxiety about returning to a place that seemed to have a degree of uncertainty around it. At the time, the whole Brexit charade was in full swing and that didn't help either. Here are some tips I would give anyone returning to work from a long absence, such as maternity leave:

Don't be so hard on yourself. Feeling guilty for not being the best parent, wife, child, employee, or friend doesn't help. Think about what you do well and what you are appreciated for.

Prioritise what is important. I love my job. However, ensuring quality time with my loved ones is a priority. All the toys in the world won't make up for spending time with the children. It is time we will never get back. I have had to choose between going to my son's Christmas production at school and attending an important CSR work event. I chose my son's school production... I wouldn't miss it for the world! Besides, life is truly too short to spend just working!

Do what works for you and your family. As parents, you constantly get advice (well-meaning intentions in most cases) from your parents, other parents, family, friends, and even strangers. It's good to listen to all advice but at the end of the day you need to do what works best for you; follow your instincts. All children are different and you need to do what's best for you, your child, and your family.

Ask and it shall be given to you. During my final keeping-in-touch-day, I was anxious about asking my new manager to have Mondays as my day off. However, when I eventually asked, he was fine with it. This shows that sometimes you can be anxious for no logical reason.

Focus on quality over quantity. Flexible working arrangements are such a life saver, which is why jobs in technology are usually fit for mums! I'm able to work from 9am to 5pm and can make up for any extra work by logging in from home in the evenings. I am lucky to have a manager who trusts me to manage my time and workload without supervision and who also values my contribution regardless of how long I physically spend in the office.

Be present. When you're with your family, truly be THERE. Listen with your mind and body and give your children and husband your full attention. That means no work e-mails, Instagram, Facebook, or Snapchat accounts. Put the phone away!

Don't take your stress out on your family. Find authentic ways to release your stress because stress and exhaustion do not make for being a good parent or employee.

You cannot control everything. Remember you cannot totally control the environment; you are not able to govern when chicken pox may strike or when the nanny might need a day off. Children love to push boundaries, especially with their parents, so do not expect them to always be well-behaved. The one thing you can control is your reaction to every situation. Ensure it's positive.

Don't take life too seriously. Sometimes you just need to let go and laugh! Being a working parent and not having family around means social life is not so straightforward. To arrange any night out or 'off' is a huge luxury. This means some evenings I might end up snuggling on the sofa watching my favourite series on Netflix with a glass of wine in hand or just giggling with my husband over stories of our most embarrassing parenting fails; laughing can be an instant energiser.

Common New Mum Mistakes to Avoid

I am yet to find a working mum that isn't worried about some aspects of combining work with children, marriage and life in general.

As soon as my first baby arrived, instead of enjoying the time with my baby as much as possible, I was preoccupied with worrying about what would happen when I eventually returned to work. I stressed so much about how much maternity leave I would take. Would I get bored and "run" back to work after 6 months? Would I take the full year? Would I need to extend the leave beyond a year? There was the worry that came with comparing his milestones with other babies. And then all the guilt about leaving the baby behind which brought me to tears on many occasion, the stress only getting worse when I struggled with breastfeeding, frequent night waking and getting into a routine.

Going back to work is another big life change many mums face, one thing that stood out for me is the fact that the way I view the world changed significantly after I became a mum. So, I thought it would be useful to share some mistakes that working mums can fall into when returning to the workplace based on my own experience but can be avoided if they knew any better.

- Being overly protective
- Not accepting help
- Relying too much on experts
- Arranging child care late
- Going Back Big Bang
- Constant mummy guilt
- Expecting no problems along the way
- Sticking to your instincts blindly

MUMMY'S CORNER

What advice would you give new mums looking to return to work after maternity leave?

Set realistic expectations of yourself. The reality is that you have moved from having one full-time job to having two full-time jobs. That can take a lot out of you if you don't balance it properly. Take some time off where you don't have the children or work to renew yourself.

I attended a maternity returner's workshop provided by my organisation which always has good pointers for transitioning back to work. I also made use of mentors who are mums themselves who have made this transition back to work. I sorted childcare well in advance and had the chance to do the settling in period before I had to return to work.

Melinda, mum of two

I would say have your diary and reminder app close to you. You don't want to overwhelm yourself thinking you're superwoman; we all need stability and time for ourselves. So take note of your monthly schedule (which may change). Ensure you agree with your boss to adjust your work pattern if required. Finally, enjoy every moment, as you know they grow up so fast!

Glory, mum of three

Be confident, and make sure you have arranged reliable childcare for your kid. Take it slowly. In the beginning, I used some holidays, which accumulated during my maternity leave, so I could work three days per week. Then I gradually increased it.

Sunny, mum of two

If your company provides Keeping In Touch Days – use them. They are a brilliant way for you to try out your new commute involving dropping off children and a good way to catch up with friends and colleagues. Coming back to work on my first official day back was nowhere near as daunting as it could have been had I not use my K.I.T Days. Believe in yourself. Your confidence can suffer when you are out of the workplace for a long time, but in fact you've been learning that whole time and will have acquired new skills and experiences that you can bring back to benefit your new work place.

Elizabeth, mum of two

My top tip is to prioritise and be organised. It will make life a little easier. Learn to say "no". Sometimes we are ashamed of saying no—especially if we are asked to stay for overtime at work. You have the right to say no and not to feel bad about it. Also, ask family members to help with things like watching your child while on a date night or girls' night out.

Melanie, mum of two

Just to go with it and do it, it gets a little easier as you go. I suffer with bad anxiety and panic attacks and the thought of a new job and leaving my daughter was the most daunting thing I have gone through, but I listened to everyone who kept telling me it gets easier. It has taken a good eight months, I would say, but I am starting to get there. It has been the hardest year of my career since I was nineteen! But now I look forward to the days where I get to have a lunchtime, catch up on things on my journey, and just have some adult conversation. I thought I would be the last person to say that, but it is true.

Kelly, mum of one

Reflection

- How did motherhood redefine you and your work?
- What can you do to ensure you don't make some of the common mistakes new mums make?
- Do you have a backup childcare in place?

Chapter Three: Standing Out at Work Sanely

Why fit in when you were born to stand out. — Dr Seuss

No matter who or where they are, women today have more opportunities than their mothers and grandmothers did. Women of today can hold jobs that were not available to women back then. More mums have full-time day jobs alongside other hobbies and interests and many even have their own businesses. For anyone questioning whether a woman can have children and a job, let's not forget Serena Williams who won the Australian Open in 2017 while she was eight weeks pregnant.

Now we're amid an emerging archetype of what motherhood can be. Women can both value their work and be good mums. The decisions I made about my corporate career and life were never easy and choosing when to 'lean in' at work versus when to focus more on my family was deeply personal. I took a year off work after having my first son whilst I took only ten months maternity leave after I had my second.

A 2015 survey by the Pew Research Center discovered that mothers who had their children at eighteen years and younger were three times more likely to complain about how difficult it was for them to advance in their job or career than the fathers. Even more problematic for mothers who have full-time jobs is the feeling of guilt and stress that come with having to divide attention between work and family.

How Do Working Mums Feel?

I wanted to find out how other mums felt about being a working mum in the 21st century, so I did some research.

MUMMY'S CORNER

What is your biggest challenge as a working mum?

The biggest challenge of my career so far is when I just returned to work after my first maternity leave. At that time, I had to bring my daughter to the city by train and then walk one hour every day to send/pick her up from the nursery. I arrived at the office at 8am and left at 5pm sharp to pick her up. My working hours were rigid and I couldn't commit a single minute of time outside of that as I needed an hour to get home, cook dinner, bathe her, put her to bed, etc.

Sunny, mum of two

My biggest challenge has to be time! I honestly think twenty-four hours in a day is not enough. My hands are so full with family, work, life, and just trying to catch my breath. I miss my precious 'me' time.

Lola, mum of two

The constant guilt of not being able to spend more time with my son because I am a working mother.

Gbemi, mum of one

Trying to avoid mistakes that will negatively affect my children; this challenge, or shall I say 'fear', manifests itself in several different forms. One of which (and perhaps at the forefront) is the guilt of being a working mum and trying to maintain a healthy work-life balance. I want to be there for every drop-off, pick-up, game, concert, and after school activity; basically, I want to give my girls 110%. Yet, somehow, I must also find a way to save a little time for myself and of course my husband. I'm a mum, wife, entrepreneur, daughter, sister, aunt, and not to forget... friend! My friends want my time too, you know.

Annabelle, mum of two

The level of organisation it takes to get the balance right. Especially with a demanding career, a large family, and young children. It's a lot of pressure mentally and physically to keep on top of it all while still making sure your family and home are your number one priority.

Bibiana, mum of three

Even though I spend the evening with my children, I don't always feel its quality time as I need to prepare dinner instead of actively interacting with them. The other thing is that sometimes when I leave in the morning my children are not awake, which makes the above even more frustrating.

Melinda, mum of two

Getting the right care for my children when I'm away from home daily and getting caregivers who are 100% trustworthy.

Tolulope, mum of four

My biggest frustration is when my child falls ill suddenly and I must take time off work. I don't enjoy begging my boss for emergency holiday.

Abby, mum of one

Managing my feelings and being able to think outside the box. What do I mean by this? Well, most mums would loath to admit this, but little people are annoying and frustrating sometimes.

Ifeyinwa, mum of five

It's my biggest frustration and my biggest lesson learnt – you can't plan anything. You never know when the children will be ill, or your best made plans will be destroyed by a two year old toddler tantrum. Whilst this is a frustration, it has helped me enormously with the way I deal with all kinds of uncertainty in life.

Elizabeth, Mum of two

It's very clear that the biggest frustration for most working mums is *time*. Working mums want more time to spend with their children and to catch up on housework.

How to Stand Out at Work

There is never enough time to do all the great things we want to achieve at work and at home. But there are several ways you can stand out in your workplace, despite being a busy mum with limited time on your hands. I believe if you follow some of these proven tips and advice, you will not only stand out at work, but you will also create the best opportunities for you to advance in your career despite of the lack of time.

Set boundaries up front
Boundaries don't keep other people out; they fence you in.

Nobody is going to usher you out of the office door at 5pm. But if that's when you have to pick up your child from school or day care, tell your employer before you start your new job. Your boss may expect you to be responsive to e-mails after working hours and it's worth considering managing this expectation. Understanding and communicating the difference between being busy and being productive is crucial to any mum's success at work. Productivity and time management Guru Tim Ferris emphasizes in his book *Four Hour Work Week* that long hours aren't a good barometer of effort, results are. Schedule empty blocks of time, which you can use to catch up on other projects and get your job done.

Be Your Authentic Self
Be yourself; everyone else is taken. —Oscar Wilde

As we spend most of our time at work, it is important that we are able to bring our whole self to work. Being ourselves is not always easy. Sometimes it means dropping the mask and being more exposed. The important thing to remember is that we always relate to people who we find to be authentic.

Shortly after I returned to my job from maternity leave the first time around, I attended a works' breakfast networking event organised by a women's network called *Women in European Business*. It aimed to help advance women's career causes. I was assigned a senior mentor during this event, an inspirational and wonderful lady who was a Managing Director and the head of Global Transaction Banking Europe Sales. She gave me the advice that just trying to fit in with the crowd and not being your authentic self would not take you far in your career.

Over time I had to learn to bring my whole and true self to work. When I first started my career, I was such a shy person that followed and blended into the crowd. I found it hard to challenge anything that didn't seem right. I couldn't disagree with senior colleagues even when I felt very strongly about my views. Moreover, whenever my colleagues (mostly male) were going out for team drinks, I tagged along even though I didn't always enjoy it. The topics they usually discussed—drinks, sports, politics, and cars—were not always my cup of tea and I found that to fit in I was just laughing at their jokes, whether I saw the humour or not.

I had to learn over time to challenge approaches or views that didn't seem right to me. I learned how to say "no" when I was not up for team drinks. Whilst it is good to socialise and network with colleagues occasionally, I would rather not hang out in the city every other night, especially when I have young children to put to bed. Now I find I can ask for a meeting to be rescheduled if the timing doesn't work for me. I can talk about the topics I care about like fashion, children, travel, and technology. I notice my colleagues and bosses respect me much more since I became assertive and confident.

Do Not Sit Quietly in Meetings

Speak up even if your voice shakes.

Don't just take notes, nod, and then leave the meeting. Listen actively and thoughtfully, ask good questions, participate, and raise concerns if you have any. Initially you might get away with being quiet in meetings, but if you want to go far in your career you're going to want to speak up at meetings. You'll come to realise your voice must be heard. You want to sound knowledgeable, so you must do your homework and research in advance. If you don't have anything to contribute, ask questions. When your boss or senior management is in a meeting with you, they take notice of all contributors. Leaders are not silent in meetings. Research shows that it's not just *how* you say something but *when* you say it that matters. We remember things best if they come at the beginning or end of a list. What gets stuck in the middle is often forgotten.

Be Credible

Do what you say you will do when you say you will do it. No one can meet every commitment they have made, but they should be able to meet most of them. I have had several situations where I didn't meet critical deliveries, but I ensured that I kept all key participants updated throughout and that meant I was rarely ever penalised. The respect you develop across the organization will, in large part, be affected by your ability to successfully and maturely manage your commitments. I have always feared being stuck in a situation where I don't know enough about the topic to discuss it intelligently. This the reason why I always do my research and prepare for meetings and to ensure I am knowledgeable about the subject. This would help to build trust with clients and stakeholders.

Always Offer Ideas and Suggestions
The best way to have a good idea is to have a lot of ideas.

Your boss and senior management want and need your ideas, but they also expect your hands to get dirty from time to time. Words don't make an organization successful; actions do. Think of ways your job can be done more effectively and efficiently and suggest recommendations for improvement. Even if your manager doesn't agree, keep making suggestions wherever you can. Anticipate problems that might arise and come up with relevant ideas to solve them. Create an improvement plan and share it with your boss. Write about your area of expertise and ideas for development in your field. Contribute to your company's website or blogs. Doing so can show others what skills you have and promote your personal brand to a wider audience. Figure out what makes you unique so you can prove you're hard to replace. Do you deliver concrete, visible results that make an impact? Are you the go-to person on a critical system or tool? If not, figure out how to become that go-to person.

Go Above and Beyond Your Role Requirements
Never stop doing your best just because someone doesn't give you credit.

Always go the extra mile in your role. Doing mediocre work won't get you noticed. To stand out, especially if your goal is promotion or to get a pay rise, you need to do outstanding work that will get you seen by your boss and other senior management. *The difference between ordinary and extraordinary is that little extra.* Look for ways you can go above and beyond daily requirements. Become an expert in something—a tool, software, or business area. People usually turn to 'perceived' experts for advice and problem solving.

Look for areas in your organization where you can put your skills to use and become an expert. Share your knowledge with others. Look at coordinating some lunch hour sessions where you will provide training to others in your area of expertise. Become the person that can be counted on to help. Don't wait for someone to approach you and avoid expecting anything in return. Help others because you want to, not because you expect something back. If you see something needs to be done and nobody else is doing it, DO IT. I am amazed by how few people do this. People who help out stand out.

When I started as a graduate trainee, I was responsible for the coffee rounds in my team. For over five years, I constantly volunteered to organise my team charity day and our team Christmas parties. This made me stand out, as everyone knew me to be a helpful person. This also meant I got to work with our CSR, compliance teams, and business managers, which in turn broadened my network and offered me exposure to other areas in the organisation.

Even though my role is a business analyst, I am more than competent to take on the role of a project manager, tester, and even developer. A senior stakeholder once asked me to prepare some statistical analysis in Excel for use at an ex-co meeting. Whilst she only asked for it in Excel format, I went ahead and prepared a PowerPoint presentation summarizing the stats. She was really impressed and told my boss what a good job I had done. It is a big deal when your boss or senior management hears positive feedback and compliments about you from your clients or stakeholders. Always assume your job is on the line—no position is ever guaranteed. This kind of attitude will keep you on your toes and make sure your CV is always up to date.

Bring Solutions with Problems

Whatever the problem, be part of the solution. Don't just sit around raising questions and pointing out obstacles. —Tina Fey

People who bring problems or habitually complain without offering solutions can become time-wasters. If you're complaining, you're not solving; you're part of the problem. When you have a problem, articulate a possible solution, offer options, and detail the specific help required. Tell your boss exactly what you need from them, such as escalation support, funding, lifting the freeze on hiring or approval of a business trip, or a new tool. You are far more likely to obtain their support when you have a recommended solution to hand over and they know precisely what is expected from them to help you carry out the solution.

Take the Lead and Lean in When You Can

Leadership belongs to those who take it. —Sheryl Sandberg

If you walk into a room and there isn't a leader—the leader is you. Even if it is not you, still contribute at a high level. Put forward ideas and suggestions. Challenge things that do not make sense. If you do this respectfully, you will stand out. Remember silence does not get you noticed; if anything, it gets you overlooked.

It's hard to be successful at your career if you only put in thirty-five hours a week. This will cause you to constantly have work time missing from your life. When required, working on weekends can help busy operational mums who want to progress their career and achieve a better balance between work and family. Take advantage of all possibilities—if your husband can take the children on the weekend while you put in some additional hours, then go for it! Success can be yours.

Professional Training and Career Development

When I read that a media agency in Shoreditch, *Brainlabs*, hired its first robot receptionist and claimed it was cheaper than a human, it got me thinking about how almost any job can be made redundant. That is why it is important to remain relevant in terms of marketable skills that provide value in changing times. Succeeding in a demanding, changing workplace requires a strategic career management plan. Employers want to attract, hire, and retain employees who provide the best value.

It's so easy to get caught up in the day-to-day duties of your job, but it's important to step back once in a while and look at the bigger picture. Some companies have formal programs to help employees develop their careers. You will need to informally pursue your career development too. A successful career doesn't happen without planning and frequent review. Here are a few ways in which you can proactively pursue your career development:

- Engage your manager in periodic discussions about your career goals. Work with him or her to create a career development plan. I have a recurring monthly meeting with my boss where we discuss my career goals and development.
- Plan to take on industry-recognized qualifications within your field.
- Attend classes and training sessions relating to technical and software skills to increase your knowledge.
- Consult the HR department to learn about career development and job opportunities, such as tuition reimbursement for a university

degree or professional certification, in-house technical or training courses, and available job openings. Take advantage of all available opportunities.
- Explore lateral moves to broaden and deepen your experience.
- Job shadowing other employees in your organization is a great way to learn about different jobs.
- Seek a mentor from a department that you would like to explore further.

Find a Career Mentor
Every great achiever is inspired by a great mentor.

I was assigned a buddy and a career mentor as part of the graduate training program when I joined my work organization. My buddy was a smart Polish guy who joined the firm a year before I did. On our first informal meeting, he showed me around Liverpool's streets, coffee shops, restaurants, and bars. He extended his network of trusted colleagues and counterparts to me so when I was seeking a placement after my first rotation, he linked me up with one of his previous managers.

My mentor, on the other hand, was a senior vice president. During our first meeting, we agreed to meet for lunch once a month. He was such a nice man but, because of his senior position, I was cautious about what I said to him. He offered me much practical advice on how to navigate such a large organization. He drew my attention to events and networks that would benefit my career aspirations. When he eventually left the organization, I got another female mentor who was a senior vice president. She continues to provide me with learning and networking opportunities in my career journey.

Self-Promotion

The difference between being an effective and successful professional is your ability to have your accomplishments recognised and rewarded. One of the most valuable lessons my first mentor taught me is that doing a good job is not enough in itself to ensure you will get ahead. If you want recognition, you need to be willing to take responsibility for broadcasting your achievements and push for appropriate rewards and advancements. In a global workplace, the message is clear; if you don't self-promote your career will likely stall.

My first career mentor advised me to keep a file of my successes, achievements, wins, and all positive feedback and thus have them at my fingertips when required. Today I still have an Excel file that contains a list of my weekly, monthly, quarterly, and yearly wins plus challenges and how I overcame them. The next step is to identify who is important to promote your success to and why. Forwarding on the appreciative or congratulatory e-mails from stakeholders or clients is a very easy way of making others aware of your success. You could write an article showcasing your expertise and knowledge in your firm's intranet or newsletter or for external publication in the professional associations.

Keep Your LinkedIn Profile Updated

LinkedIn has become an incredibly powerful job hunting and virtual networking tool. In just five minutes you can forge connections, endorse performances of colleagues, and add to your list of potential clients and colleagues. Instead of rushing around when you're ready for a job jump, take time to hone your profile on a regular basis; even if you absolutely love and feel secure in your job, it could provide you with additional opportunities to promote yourself, like publishing posts or articles that boost your position as an expert in your field.

MUMMY'S CORNER

How can you stand out as a working mum?

Never use your children as an excuse for absence or not getting things done. Don't be antisocial; participate in social and community activities. Perform over and beyond your role. Be willing to take on more and never compromise on quality.

Olivia, mum of four

If you want to keep progressing in your career, avoid long career breaks. Focus on quality over quantity. The children will be fine without you 24/7.

Dr Monica, mum of three

My top tip is to not try to be a different person at work to the one you are at home. I don't think I stand out, despite being a busy working mum. Being a parent has made me truly understand the importance of setting clear expectations and straightforward feedback. It's also made me utterly intolerant of spending time on things that don't move the ball forward.

Elly, mum of three

To stand out at work, deliver business and organization goals. Be result centric, not activity based.

Tolulope, mum of four

Being a mum is not something I can switch on or off; nevertheless, being a professional is having the ability to not allow one area of your personal life to have a negative impact on your professional life. As a mum, I might not have the liberty to stay late at work or go to every networking evening. I might not be as motivated to progress in my career the way I wanted to prior to becoming a mum but standing out in the work place is me giving my absolute best. As a mum, I can leverage the innate and acquired skills, and these can make me stand out. My organisation skills will certainly get me noticed, as I can show that, despite the contrary, I am more than able. The ability to multi-task when required; to complete tasks and go beyond the call of duty.

Bimbola, mum of four

I try to make sure that I get involved in as many social situations as I can. Becoming a working mum, you find you just want to get home and be back in your bubble with your new baby. But having done this for the first few months, I felt excluded a bit and being part-time did not help. So, I try and attend social drinks/team events when I can to stay in contact. Another thing is I make sure that if there are childcare problems, my daughter is ill, or for any reason it stops me coming in, I will make sure I am available at home to log on when I can.

Kelly, mum of one

By doing your work well. Prior to coming back to work from maternity leave, I kept in touch with work by checking in regularly with my bosses and colleagues. I brushed off my skills and knowledge because I wanted to come back with a bang; I didn't want my colleagues to give me passes because i was a new working mum. Slowly but surely, I was able to improve upon my deliverables.

Abosede, mum of three

I do my best to be present in each role. When I am at work, I focus on doing amazing work there and when I am working on passion projects, I do the same. When I plan for each year, I make sure I have growth goals in all the different areas of my life that matter to me.

Abi, mum of two

From Self-Doubt to Self-Confidence

Confidence is not "They will like me". Confidence is "I'll be fine I they don't".
— Christina Grimme

When I first arrived in the United Kingdom, I was comfortable with having my Nigerian accent because I was studying at a University alongside many international students with differing and similar accents to me. For one thing, having an accent can enable you to stand out. As your accent comes out naturally in conversation, people take interest in where you are from and your cultural background. It can be a great conversation starter when you meet new people.

It was not until after my first maternity leave that I became self-conscious of my then relatively hybrid Nigerian-British accent. I recall phoning a senior stakeholder based in New York to explain changes the development team had made to one of the systems I supported. He asked me where my accent was from, as he did not recognize it. I explained I was born and raised in Nigeria and relocated to the United Kingdom after my degree. Being a migrant can be amazing sometimes, as you're super proud of your heritage, but when you're trying to have regular intellectual conversations without having to explain where you were born or where you grew up or where your parents are from, those are the times you wish you could just have a good old British accent or your name was Jane Doe. That conversation seemed to be the trigger. From that point onwards, I started doubting my abilities and my self-confidence took a huge hit. It got so bad I couldn't even speak up in group meetings and workshops even though I knew what I was talking about. I was an expert at my job, hence knowledge was not the issue. It took time for me to rebuild my self-confidence.

I had to apologetically 'warn' new stakeholders I had an accent or else run the risk of continually repeating myself, particularly on the phone, due to my being more self-conscious. When the person you're talking to is expecting a British accent, it makes sense that it takes them time to adjust to the way you speak. I had to reach a place where I saw my hybrid accent as that of a super-special bicultural queen rather than an oddity.

Many women struggle with post-baby weight, knowledge gaps, or fear. Regardless of the reason for your low self-confidence, it is clear this negative emotional block will hold you back from achieving your potential. It can cause you to miss out on many opportunities and leave you with a less than happy, satisfying, and fulfilling life. The good news according to Eleanor Roosevelt is no one can make you feel inferior without your consent. No one in the world has the power to make you feel less than them, the only person that holds that ability is you. Therefore you can learn to rebuild self-confidence.

Mastering self-confidence can help you on the path to success in your career and beyond. Here are some actions that can help build your self-confidence.

Get Prepared

Proper preparation prevents poor performance.

It's hard to be confident in yourself if you don't think you'll do well at something. Beat that feeling by preparing yourself as much as possible. For example, think about delivering a presentation; if you haven't prepared your slides, you won't have confidence and believe in yourself to deliver a good presentation. But if you set time to prepare and sufficiently practice your delivery and responses to imagined questions, you'll look and feel confident. Your confidence will receive a huge boost when you have done your homework and appropriately prepared yourself for that workshop. Do not underestimate the power of preparation in giving you the self-confidence you seek.

Increase Your Knowledge

Increasing your knowledge is another great strategy for building self-confidence. It might seem obvious, but you can build confidence by learning more. Read relevant technical and expertise books relating to your field of expertise. Watch useful TED Talks. Attend professional seminars and networking events. A point of caution: it's easy to go overboard and spouting your knowledge too often can be a confidence killer when people who have greater knowledge on the subject start debating with you. Knowing what to do about a complex issue or problem can help confidence. Confidence grows when you act on what you know.

Dress Nicely and Groom Yourself

If you dress nicely, you'll feel good about yourself. You'll feel confident, presentable, and ready to tackle the world. Dressing nicely means something different for everyone. It doesn't necessarily mean wearing a £200 tailored dress. It could mean wearing business smart outfits that are nice looking and presentable. Getting your nails manicured and applying light makeup can contribute toward feelings of self-confidence. There have been days when I turned my mood around completely just by getting a French manicure.

Speak with a Deliberate Voice

Effective communication is 20% what you know and 80% how you feel about what you know. —Jim Rohn

I had to rebuild my self-confidence by learning to speak loud and clear. A weak, unsure, or timid voice will not help your cause. Avoid mumbling; use a strong, resolute, and passionate voice. Speak slow enough to ensure you are not only heard but also understood. Engage others in your conversation, participate in meetings, ask questions, answer questions, and give feedback. Your voice must always be heard. Don't beat yourself up if you don't initially get it right. Your posture and the manner you engage with others can send a strong message that says you are engaged, ready for action, and committed to the dialogue. For example, sit upright with your chin up. If standing, stand upright with your shoulders back. With people from most cultures, give direct eye contact. Move your head, body, and arms when in discussion or listening to someone. Use open gestures and lean forward for emphasis. Don't cower or withdraw. Shake hands firmly; avoid a limp handshake. Be generous with your smile.

Think Positive

Tell the negative committee that meets inside your head to sit down and shut up. — Ann Bradford

You become what you think about all day long. Give yourself respect and have positive thoughts. Through your thoughts and actions, you create a self-fulfilling prophecy. The self-talk can come from your inner thoughts, your actual words, notes and messages to yourself, and any other form of self-communication. Don't be so hard on yourself. Be honest and truthful, but also cut yourself some slack. We are all work in progress with plenty of room for improvement. Self-confidence can be learned, practiced, and become a core part of who you choose to be. Self-confidence is largely what you think about yourself along with your knowledge, skills, and experiences you have worked hard to acquire.

Bounce the Criticism

What others think about you is none of your business. — Jack Canfield

It is far less important what others think about you than what you think about yourself. Listen to what people say because you can learn from it and move on. If you give more weight to what others think about you than what you think about yourself, you are giving control of yourself to others. Don't give that power away. Never allow your source of self-confidence to come from someone else. If you hear something negative about yourself that isn't true, simply reject it. Don't dwell on it or allow it to destroy your self-confidence. Try thinking of something more positive and remind yourself about the skills you do have and how unique you are.

Avoid Being Around Negative People

Don't give your energy away to toxic people. — Robert Few

People who put you down, are constantly critical of you, or behave destructively towards you can cause self-doubt and pull you down. If you frequently experience put-downs, harsh criticism, and outright nasty and rude behaviors, your self-confidence could easily come into doubt. This situation adds no value to your career and can also prevent you from developing into the best version of you. If you tend to hang out with people who criticize you, that's going to kill your confidence. It might be time to find new associates.

One of my work colleagues, a lovely lady I met when I started my career. She always has a nice compliment for me—she continually praises how I dress and style my hair. This is a constant form of confidence boost and it is so valuable.

MUMMY'S CORNER

What is your top tip for boosting self-confidence at work?

Knowledge; improve your knowledge of your function or domain to be seen as the go-to person and expert. Take on your fear, whether it be public speaking or presentation.

Olivia, mum of four

I come from the school of thought that says, 'If you don't believe and be confident in yourself, no one will'. I work daily on myself, first by believing in myself and never doubting what I am capable of. I spend my emotions and energy on things that will add value to my life, paying little or no attention to things that distract me from achieving my goals. Life is very challenging; therefore, I choose to focus on things that elevate and add value to my existence.

Jo, mum of three

Confidence can come from few places. If you are a Christian and you believe in God, you would know that He created you for a purpose and be rest assured that you've got backing from Him. Secondly, when you know what you're doing in terms of knowledge and skills, it helps with confidence. And finally, believe in yourself.

Abosede, mum of three

How to Be More Efficient at Work

I love running high profile projects, hitting milestones, and meeting delivery deadlines. At the same time, I love coming home to my children and cuddling them at bedtime. Being efficient simply means working in a well-organized, systematic, productive, and competent way. It entails re-focusing your schedule and completing tasks. It is important to manage expectations and communicate regularly with whomever your work would impact upon. So, with the mission in mind of being productive at work to ensure all commitments are met but not being completely burnt out by the end of the working week, I've put together some simple and effective tips on how to achieve this.

Prioritize and Maintain a Master To-Do List

Draw up a daily to-do list, either at the start of the day or ideally at the end of the previous work day. Identify your top three priority tasks that should be worked on each day. Resist allowing low-value tasks to consume significant amounts of your time. Break larger tasks into smaller ones and you will gain a sense of accomplishment as tasks are individually completed. I usually check my work diary before I leave work in the evening and write down my priorities for the next day.

Use a Technique for Assigning Priorities to Tasks

Many mums ask me, "How do I know how to prioritize what needs to be done?" Although there are many techniques to help with effective work prioritization, I have adapted the popular 'Time Management Matrix' by Stephen Covey from his book *The Seven Habits of Highly Effective People*. The Time Management Matrix is useful when it is tough to gauge which tasks are more important. It is represented as a box with four quadrants and it distinguishes between importance and urgency. Important tasks are those that contribute to the achievement of your goals and create the highest value. Urgent tasks are those that require immediate attention. Your high priority items should be tasks that fall within the Important and urgent grid as reflected in the table below.

	URGENT	NOT URGENT
Important	**Quadrant I Do It Now** - Emergencies e.g. regulator unscheduled visit - Crisis e.g. production issue - Last minute Preparations - Last minute assignment from boss - Pressing important meetings - Important deadlines - Deadline driven projects - Pressing problems - Escalations	**Quadrant II (Decide when to do it)** - Planned presentation or Meeting - Long-term Strategy and Planning - Relationship Building - Stakeholder Management - Professional development - Training - Recreation and Wellness - Proactive measures - Continuous improvements
Not Important	**Quadrant II (Delegate)** - Some emails and Meetings - Some Reports and Presentations - Interruptions and Distractions - Dealing with others' request	**Quadrant II (Dump it** - Busy Work - Trivial Work - Junk Email - Some Hone calls - Any time wasting activity - Workplace gossip

Avoid Multi-Tasking-Multi-tasking can lead to time wasting when energy has to be re-focused or mistakes have to be fixed. Attempting to manage several tasks at once may decrease performance levels.

Check Your Progress- Constantly check-in with yourself to assess how you are getting on with your tasks and if what you are doing is productive.

Delegate- Break down a task and empower others to contribute effort. Consider only attending meetings that will reveal information you need or when you have information someone else needs.

Reserve Some 'Me Time' Each Day- Use this quiet time to relax; be mindful and re-energize. Learn to accept 'good enough' where acceptable to ensure you don't get burnt out trying to attain perfection.

MUMMY'S CORNER

What is your top tip for being effective and productive in the office?

I make lists. I have a notebook that is marked out with coloured tabs to divide it into sections and I find writing down all my ideas, things to do, plan for promotion, etc. really helps me stay focused. I am very busy with a three-year-old and am pregnant with my second, so baby brain is well and truly here, which is why being organized keeps me sane!
Emma Reed, mum of two

Focus on one thing at a time rather than trying to get everything done at once. Stop multi-tasking. I turn my mobile off for a couple of hours at a time,

> otherwise I find I am constantly checking it.
>
> **Funmi, mum of two**
>
> Look at tomorrow's agenda before leaving the office. It helps focus your mind for the next day and to ensure you have everything ready for an important meeting.
>
> **Kelly, mum of two**

Jobs that Support Working from Home

Sheryl Sandberg's book *Lean In* revealed 43% highly qualified women are leaving their careers due to family commitments. This causes a huge waste of talent on top of the loss of income. One gap I found in her book was the lack of advice or strategy for mums looking to re-enter the workforce.

My previous job as Application Developer for a medium-sized IT education company provided remote technology that offered me the ability to do my job from home. My current job within the corporate Investment Banking sector also supports flexible and remote working. Many well-established employers embrace flexible working as it increasingly suits the modern workforce, which will be highly beneficial to many mums with young children. Most women would consider their childcare responsibilities before changing roles or applying for a new job or promotion. Plus, access to flexibility at work is usually linked to salary and seniority, with those on lower incomes being the least able to work flexibly. With a new employer, it can be difficult to begin a conversation about flexible working; however, if you are looking for a job where the employer embraces flexible working as part of their culture, most

IT jobs in organizations such as large corporations and start-ups usually support working from home.

In 2013 during a visit to see my sister in San Francisco, we went to check out the Facebook headquarters in Silicon Valley. How rhetorical their address was: *1 Hacker Way*. Whilst at the headquarters, I observed many employees having a run around their campus in the middle of the day. Their office looked very cool with sleeping pods, snooker tables, and gaming stations. They had a gym with private trainers and a launderette service to name but a few of their employee perks. However, as generous as the incentives looked from the outside, it appeared to me those organizations wanted to keep you in the office 24/7. These generous workplace perks wouldn't appeal to everyone (especially at my age), as I would still like to go home to my children. I wouldn't want to have an evening nap in the office no matter how cool the office space was.

Many women with babies and young children have asked me which jobs tend to offer flexible and work-from-home options. Here are some IT related jobs I know are more likely to support working from home.

1. Application Tester
2. Project Management
3. Project Management Analyst
4. Project Support Officer
5. Database Architect
6. Software Engineer
7. User Experience Designer
8. Business Analyst

9. Product Owner
10. Scrum Master
11. Application Support Engineer
12. Data Entry Specialist
13. Database Engineer
14. Digital Product Manager
15. Research Analyst
16. Financial Analyst
17. IT Auditor
18. Social Media Manager

What Does a Mum-Friendly Workplace Entail?

The comments from the mums on their biggest challenges show how important it is to work for an employer that not only supports flexible working but also understands the problems and challenges women face today. The mom friendly organizations are helping women thrive in the workplace in terms of providing flexible working, paid leave, and support for career advancement.

Some offer fully paid maternity leave and the majority also offer flexi-time, back-up childcare, professional development opportunities for women, mentoring programs, and career counselling.

Dressing for Success

Never underestimate the power of a good outfit on a bad day.

Your personal style reflects your image and people tend to judge you by the way you look. We've all heard the sayings *'dress for the job you want, not the job you have'* and *'dress the way you want to be addressed'*. I recall our executive career coach at work saying the biggest problem most of her clients face is creating a 'coherent executive presence'.

An effective mum should aim to look smart, confident, and put together even whilst holding a baby in one hand and a nappy bag in the other. Since becoming a mum, I have adopted the 'minimalist' style. It is about making an effort and putting a lot of thought into it but making sure it looks effortless. The idea is to look good while also looking like you're not trying at all.

No matter what the dress code is in your organization, business formal, smart casual, or casual, you should always look well turned out. Your clothes should continually look neat and clean. Apart from boosting your self-esteem and confidence, you never know who you may run into.

To keep up with this trend, I had to build a wardrobe that combined casual with chic and comfortable with professional. Being a working mum doesn't mean you can't look smart, stylish, and chic. Bear in mind you have to spend long hours working and attending meetings. What you wear is your choice, but aim to keep things stylish without compromising on comfort. In many instances, I have taken my heel height down from three inches to one inch; I usually wear comfortable trainers during my commute into work. Here are some tips for anyone looking to boost their work wardrobe:

Stay True to Yourself

It is key to think wisely before buying any clothing items. The first thing to consider is how to fit that individual item into your existing wardrobe. Classic style is not just about great or expensive items but about how one puts them together. A true style icon never buys clothes randomly and tosses them into her wardrobe. She carefully crafts her closet based on her personal style.

Trends are great to experiment with but it is imperative to develop your signature style based on what you know to be your true individual and aesthetic identity. Dress for you and buy what you like. Don't wear something just because it's popular or in season. Experiment with trends only after you've invested in what suits you first. Be you. If you dress in a way that makes you feel positive, confidence will exude from inside and you'll look good no matter what you're wearing.

Maintain Your Wardrobe Basics

Figure out what your work essentials are, be it a black-tailored blazer, white and black blouses, a little black dress, high pump heels, black flats, red lipstick, diamond studs, and anything else that has a central role in your personal work style. It is smarter to spend a little more on a few good quality items than having a bunch of poor quality stuff that would require you spending more to repair or replace them.

- Scarves will not only keep you warm on colder days but will also help add a bit of quotient style into your ordinary everyday wear.
- Get at least one pair of quality and classy footwear. You can buy some ballerinas, flats, or black pumps; most of them go well with almost every dress so you can look elegant every day. Nude heels matched to your skin tone are always a safe bet and they make your legs look longer. You don't need to wear high heels every time. Instead, buy shoes that look elegant and can be worn on any occasion.
- Always go for at least one stylish coat. Some people may only see you in your coat, so if you're not wearing something great underneath your military wool or trench coat, they'll never know.

- Working mums usually won't have time for ironing, so avoid buying clothes that need to be ironed.
- Be mindful of keeping your outfits appropriate for what the day ahead will bring. Dressing for the weather not only keeps you comfortable but allows you to maintain your wardrobe with those essential seasonal trends.

Keep Make-Up Simple

Most busy mums do not have time to apply heavy make-up that comprises of false lashes and layers of foundation and powder; however, just five minutes on a routine will make a world of difference and project a polished image to the outside world. It is a good idea to keep your make-up simple and subtle (again, less is more). You can apply concealer underneath your eyes to hide any dark circles or under-eye bags and then a mineral powder foundation that can provide the coverage of a foundation with the comfort of a powder. You can add a bit of bronzer, blusher, and black mascara and in addition a lip gloss or lipstick will give a simple yet stylish finish to your overall look. With make-up in place, you are ready to step out.

Work Clothes Need Not Be Dull

Just because you have to dress in formal or semi-business attire to work, it doesn't mean you have to sacrifice style. Find well-tailored pieces and incorporate accessories and colour to create a more exciting look. Even if you're not a fan of wearing bright colours, try including a hint of colour into your outfit; colour can bring your whole look together and turn a simple 'cute' outfit into something eye-catching.

If You Feel Uncomfortable, Give it a Pass

Your confidence can be affected by what you wear, so if you're feeling self-conscious about your outfit with the nagging intuitive thought that you're likely to be tugging or double-checking everything is in place all the time, maybe wear something more suited and more comfortable. If the weather is cold, always have a stylish jacket or sweater with you. In a nutshell, if your outfit makes you feel uncomfortable, ditch it.

Wear Nice Underwear

Wearing nice underwear every day will make you feel special and boost your confidence. Be sure to get your bras fitted every now and then; this will make your clothes hang better in the right places and be more comfortable—and thank goodness for Spanx that allow you to breathe whilst wearing a body shaper. Body shapers are ideal for hiding mummy tummy excess bulge and allow clothes to glide on smoothly.

Smiles are Always in Fashion

You are never fully dressed without a smile; it's the most inexpensive way to improve your looks.

"How Would You Describe Your Personal Style?"

If it is casual, I will go with leggings or jeans with a t-shirt. I can always dress this outfit up with stylish jewellery, shoes, and a cardigan. I also love throwing dresses on because they are so easy and comfortable to wear.

Kayla, mum of one

When putting an outfit together, my number one rule is to ask, "What is the vibe?" Wherever you're going, what is the atmosphere likely to be? Are people relaxed and having a good time? Or is it an important meeting and you want to make a good impression? Dress according to the 'feel' of the event or location. My personal style has changed since becoming a mother. It is more conservative and I gravitate toward pieces I can wear at work and on weekends. I don't have a lot of 'night out' clothing anymore. Work clothes can usually be paired with jeans or more casual clothes to look 'put' together on the weekends.

Pamela, mum of three

For Mums Looking to Re-Enter the Workforce

Opting out of work to raise your children doesn't have to be the end of your career. For mums that decide to stay at home or extend their maternity leave, it is always possible to get back to work at a later date; you might just need advice and inspiration. Remember, as a full-time mum, you opted to do the most important job in the world—to raise the next generation of capable, responsible adults.

But now the children are a bit older and you have the desire to pursue other passions. You may be ready to re-enter the workforce. Whilst job hunting may seem like a daunting task (do you even have a copy of your CV anymore?), these tips will give you guidance as you begin your back-to-work journey:

Perform a Self-Evaluation

Whether you've been out work for two or ten years, you need to think carefully about what your reason is for wanting to return to work. Are you going back for the money? Are you going back to be in the presence of other adults? Or are you returning because you want to find more meaning in your life? Your reasons for returning to work at this stage in your life may differ from those that drove you in your pre-baby years.

Many women don't want to go back to the high-powered, high-stress job they had before children. Your shifting priorities may necessitate pursuing a less traditional career or a completely new route. You may care more about flexibility and work-life balance than a huge salary. Take time to figure out what matters most. You might be willing to push for a high-profile role if your children are older. What skills do you have? What skills do you need? Perform an honest self-assessment. Don't rush this step. Try doing this on your own or with your spouse and/or a career coach. Once you've completed your self-evaluation, read some job descriptions of roles and positions you would be interested in pursuing to identify your strengths, weaknesses, and areas for improvements.

Explore Volunteer Opportunities

Your time at home with children can be a great time to dabble in different interests and possible career paths. You can do this by volunteering in fields that interest you. For example, if you are thinking about entering the education sector, you can volunteer on the PTA committee or as a school governor at your child's school. If you want to become a writer, you can volunteer to write for a local council, church website, or a blog. If you want to go into marketing and events management, you can volunteer to arrange a fundraising event for a local charity or organise a school event at your child's school or day care centre.

Go for coffee with friends and acquaintances that work in fields which are of interest to you; pick their brains and ask questions like: How did you get started? What do you like and dislike about your job? What skills does one need to perform your job? If you want to go back to your pre-child profession, seek out volunteer opportunities in that field to help rebuild your CV.

Update Your Skills

Based on your self-evaluation, you can identify the marketable skills you need to build or improve upon relevant to your chosen career aspirations.

Try to learn everything about the role you're interested in. Read books and white papers, attend webinars, seminars and conferences. Speak to people in and around the profession. How familiar are you with the latest version of MS Word, Excel, and PowerPoint? What about connectivity tools such as Skype and Outlook? Now is the time to brush up on your computer skills. Visit relevant job sites such as Monster, Totaljobs, JobServe or go directly to the company website to find out what skills are required for the jobs you're interested in. Learn or relearn the necessary skills! You can find classes—some free or at minimal cost—at local libraries, community colleges, and online.

If your chosen career path is an expertise route, it might be useful to work towards acquiring an industry-recognised qualification when entering the job market. For example, for project management roles, the PRINCE2 foundation qualification is highly recognised in the United Kingdom and this will make you stand out from your competitors when faced with an interview. Some other expertise roles, such as HR executive or business management, might also require you to work toward obtaining an additional degree such as a CIPD, Bachelor's, Master's, or MBA programme.

Update Your CV

As a stay-at-home mum, you most likely have a large gap in your CV, so you'll need to figure out how to fill the gap with the skills and experience you've acquired during your time out of work. Most mums have spent a good deal of time volunteering, whether at their children's school or in the community. Volunteering is great. It keeps your experience relevant, shows you are proactive, and brings you into contact with references and networking opportunities. Did you raise thousands of pounds for your kid's school to renovate their school hall? Did you serve on a committee or a board? If you helped update the school's website or do PR for a friend, you can add these to your CV as pro bono consulting projects. By doing this, you can still get credit for all the unpaid work you have done during your stay-at-home years.

You will want to create or update your LinkedIn and Facebook profiles as well as your personal website, if you have one. Below are some general CV tips:

- When it comes to CVs, one size doesn't fit all. Everything you include must be completely tailored to the organisation and role you're applying for. Include all relevant experiences, paid or voluntary. This will make it easier for them to see that you're the perfect candidate.
- An error-free CV is vital in showcasing your precision and attention to detail, so check everything—even your contact details. Spelling is crucial.

- Don't put anything on your CV that you won't be able to defend at interview. There is nothing worse than being asked questions you're unable to answer.
- Recruiters on average spend about eight seconds looking at any one CV and a sure-fire way of landing yourself on the 'no' pile is to send them your entire life story. Your CV shouldn't be longer than two A4-size pages.
- 'Role Relevant' keywords and buzzwords are very important, as they will help search engines pick out your CV from the pile.

Look for Mum-Friendly Jobs

If you are looking for an employer who permits flexible working arrangements, do your research properly. Check out the mom-friendly companies list from the *Working Mother* website to identify potential companies that recruit into your chosen field. Try connecting with current or former employees on LinkedIn or do a Google search for any articles about whether an employer promotes work-life balance or has won any awards for this recognition. If there aren't policies on the company website about work-life balance, the company probably does not allow flexible arrangements as a recruitment tool.

There are several websites and women's networks that help mums who are trying to pre-launch their careers, whether they're seeking a traditional 9-5 job or a more flexible or part-time work arrangement. Professional networks, such as Women Returners Professional Network and We Are the City, are strongly motivated to support women in developing satisfying careers that include (maternal) breaks and helping women move forward confidently. They also provide the tools mums need to revamp their CVs, answer tough questions about career gaps, and negotiate flexibility.

Additionally, many corporate multi-national organisations such as Vodafone, Santander, Accenture, PwC, MasterCard, and Credit Suisse Bank of America, usually have return-to-work schemes tailored to women returners. You can search these opportunities on their respective company websites ensuring you take note of their application timelines.

Job Sites and Networking

When it comes to the general job market, you will need to do your research to establish the best place to apply for the type of industry job you want. In Nigeria, Jobberman and ngcareers are popular jobsites. In the United Kingdom, there are many general job sites such as Reed, Indeed, and Totaljobs. For IT jobs, JobServe is the most popular tool. Many women also use recruitment agencies if they want to apply for expert roles. You can select a list of companies you're interested in working for and apply directly via their careers sites.

According to the Office of National Statistics, 70% of all jobs are still found through networking. The same people you've been working with through volunteering, chatting with at play dates, and calling for parenting advice may be critical to your job search. Let them know you are looking for work. You may be surprised by the kind of job opportunities that turn up when your network is helping you search.

If you belong or used to belong to a professional association, such as the British Computer Society or Chartered Financial Analyst Institute, visit its website for career assistance. Are you a university alumnus? Contact the career services office at your alma mater—many universities have online career networks where you can find alumni who would be thrilled to help with your job search.

Try to follow up as many times as necessary to find out if your connections know of any opportunities until you get a response. Double check their timeline and remind them you will reach out if you don't hear anything.

Top Tip: Don't keep your job search a secret. Tell everyone you want to go back into work.

Leverage LinkedIn

The most common thing recruiters and hiring mangers do after reading your CV is check your LinkedIn page, if you have one. Hence, it is crucial that you update your LinkedIn profile so it demonstrates all the positive attributes you've expressed in your CV while also telling a story that compels a prospective employer to reach out.

Use a professional photo and a well-crafted bio that encapsulates your professional history and shows what you are passionate about in a condensed manner. You should regularly add to your list of connections and ask for recommendations from colleagues and former managers. At the very least, your LinkedIn Bio should include wording which reflects that you're currently seeking new opportunities; this will ensure recruiters find you more easily.

I would also recommend the LinkedIn Premium, which allows you to send direct InMail messages to most LinkedIn user with no previous connection necessary; it also provides more tools to help your profile stand out to recruiters.

Many users, especially at the executive level, maintain privacy settings that restrict users from connecting with them. InMails are a great way to get the attention of people outside your network by giving you an otherwise forbidden ability to send private messages to recruiters, hiring managers, and senior executives.

Top Tip: Recruiters are more likely to respond to a LinkedIn InMail message from those outside their network.

How to Dress for a Job Interview

Dressing professionally shows respect for yourself, the interviewer, and the company. You may not have to dress like this every day, but you are more likely to be taken seriously when you present yourself in a neat and professional manner. In addition to following the general rules for workplace attire previously mentioned, here are additional tips on dressing for a job interview:

- Always dress slightly better for a job interview than you would if you were an employee. Dress in a manner that is professionally appropriate to the position for which you are applying. In almost all cases, this means wearing a suit. It is rarely appropriate to 'dress down' for an interview, regardless of company dress code policy. When in doubt, wear a suit.ABlouseWear a conservative blouse with your suit. Avoid wearing bright colours or anything indecent.
- If casual clothing is allowed, for example jeans and t-shirts, you should take it up a notch and put on a nice pair of pants and a button-down shirt. After all, this is a special occasion and you always want to look your best.
- Cover up tattoos and remove body jewellery until you know whether they are acceptable. If you usually dye your hair unusual colours, you may want to go back to your natural hair colour for the interview.

- Avoid strong and overpowering perfume. Make sure you have fresh breath. Your hair should be neat, clean, and conservative.
- Make-up and nail polish should be conservative or neutral. Avoid bright colours or very long nails.

Reflection

- What is your biggest challenge at work right now? What circumstances makes you want to give up your career?
- Perform a SWOT (Strengths, Weakness, Opportunities ad Threats) analysis on yourself, your skills, knowledge and experience to identify your strengths, weakness and determine areas for improvement.
- How will you go about broadening your understanding and seeking new challenges?
- Do you have a work mentor you can reach out to for career advice?

Chapter Four: Organizing Your Home Life

But everything should be done in a fitting and orderly manner. — I Corinthians 14:40

Even before I had children, I was always into planning and staying abreast of everything. Then the children came along and it was thrown into a little bit of chaos. However, I have since found ways to be an organised mum that works for me. Nowadays, I hardly ever walk in the door in the evening feeling overwhelmed because I know exactly what needs to be done and I do it.

Before it went to administration, BHS was one of my favourite home stores. I used to buy most of my children's clothes, household furnishings, beddings, and kitchen utensils there as it was conveniently located near my house. It was such a shame to see the company went into administration. On one of my shopping visits (I was working from home on this day), I logged off work at 5pm and had an hour bandwidth before having to pick my son up from the nursery. I decided to use the time to pick up a few things I ordered online from BHS.

The sales advisor, a fantastic lady, probably in her late forties, was very friendly and asked me what I did for a living. I told her about my job and how it enables me to work flexibly and remotely from home on certain 'set' days. I further explained how this allowed me to dash to the local stores after I finished my work for the day. She was truly astonished, as she hadn't heard much about the concept of remote working. On exiting BHS, I checked my to-do list on my phone and saw that a friend's daughter's birthday was in a few days' time, so I dashed into Card Factory to buy a card. I still made it in time to pick up my son at 6pm. It's crazy how much you can achieve in any given hour once you become a working mum. In a nutshell, this is what organizing my home looks like.

Let's face it, being a working mum can be extremely challenging. It takes a lot of planning and support to manage a household. As a working mum, you can go from wife to mum to cleaner to cook to employee to shopper to sister to friend, all in one day. With all these hats to wear, if you don't stay focused and organized you will end up getting burnt out. Not only can clutter in the home cause stress, it can also affect your physical health, relationships, career, and finances. Clutter can also threaten your safety and that of your children. Children living in a severely cluttered environment are less happy and are more likely to feel embarrassed about their home's condition.

Sometimes, however, we set unattainable standards of being perfect 'Pinterest' mothers whilst also striving for a 'shattered glass ceiling' and high-flying career or business. It is no secret that it takes a tremendous amount of effort to balance family life, work, cleaning, cooking, and your own interests and hobbies.

Every working mother faces her own set of unique challenges and circumstances. It can be such a struggle wondering if you are doing the right thing and considering how you'll manage to get everything done. In the end, you will have to work out an approach that suits you best. In her book *I Know How She Does It: How Successful Women Make the Most of Their Time*, Laura Vanderkam gives some tools that can help us make time for everything that's important and cut out what's not.

Efficient mums usually get more done before 7am or after 9pm than most people do all day. They know the time to get serious about getting things done is when the children are asleep. So, if you want to be efficient, pick the time of day that's most productive for you and guard that time. Just remember burning the candle at both ends only leads to burn-out. Pick one or the other and still make a good night's sleep a priority.

One of the biggest secrets to being a successful working mum and not losing your sanity is being honest with yourself about your limits; ask for assistance and get help when needed. I've put together some simple tips to help stay organized as a busy working mum:

Decide on Your Priorities

You simply can't do it all at once by yourself.

Just like your work tasks, decide on the top five things around your home that make a difference in how everyone functions and focus on getting those things done each week. These top five things can and will change depending on your circumstances. Find a scheduling system that works with your family. My husband and I use a shared Google calendar for all major events and we synchronise this with reminder alarms on our phones. We also have a family wall calendar that has individual sections for everyone plus a daily/weekly to-do list. I have created a monthly planner to help you stay organized as a busy mum. You can make a copy, pin it on the wall or on your fridge door and use it to record and capture important events for the month. It can be updated as plans and schedule change. You won't have any reason not to be organized anymore. You can find a copy of my monthly planner in the back of this book.

Be Proactive

Dig the well before you are thirsty. **—Chinese proverb**

Effective working mums should try and avoid running out of key supplies such as nappies, tooth paste, toilet rolls, or anti-bacterial wipes. Being in a house with a small child or two means anything can happen at any time and, therefore, you need sufficient cleaning materials, medical supplies, and crafting provisions as well as a good stock of food and groceries. A few times a year, I usually buy a pack of £1 birthday cards from Card Factory and store them away. I also stock up on disposable plates, cups, napkins, wrapping paper, and other assorted goods for family celebrations and birthday parties. When the 'book people' come to the office to sell their books, I stock up on numerous discounted children's books. All of this comes in handy when it's yet another child's party. If a nice toy is on sale at any of the supermarket chains, I will buy up to three and store them. A few months before my eldest son's first birthday party, I managed to get a discount voucher for our local leisure centre where my son had his tots swim lessons. This saved me 25% off booking the function room for his celebration party.

Make a list of recurring purchases and stock up once a month on the most important of these. Review your list every fortnight, or thereabouts, and order/buy anything you are running low on. This always helps not having to run around at the last minute. Where possible, make use of online shopping and next-day delivery. Every now and then, I order in bulk from ASDA online or go to the store on a weeknight to do my bulk purchasing. The stores are less crowded later in the evening. The less time you spend shopping, the more time you have to do the things you love.

A Clean House

Instead of cleaning my house I will just watch an episode of hoarders and think wow my house looks great!

It can be hard to have a clean and tidy home when you have a toddler running around. The truth is that neat and tidy surroundings are a key component in being efficient. It is up to you to decide whether you have the required bandwidth to take on cleaning responsibilities in your home or whether you need to outsource aspects of it.

Up until my first maternity leave, we never used any cleaning services within the household. My husband loves to clean and I can clean as well even though I have never enjoyed cleaning. But then came a period where I was hosting a baby shower at our house for around twenty-five people; I wasn't content to give up my sleep to tidy up after the party, which ended very late, so I found a cleaning company to come the next morning. From that day on, I've become a great believer in cleaning services and the value they provide.

To have people come into your home and sweep your floors, deep clean your kitchen, deep clean your bathrooms, vacuum, polish the furniture, clean glass and mirrors, sanitise your microwave, wipe down all surfaces, and leave your home looking spotless and smelling so clean is priceless.

Whether it's a weekly maintenance or a monthly deep clean, hiring help will allow you to spend more time with your family, which, in turn, will help you feel better about all the hours missed while you're at work. I have also been fortunate enough that my weekday nannies help with the cleaning. I am happier and calmer when my home is organized and clean. Instead of having to spend time on cleaning every day, we can just get on with the 'light' tasks like making the beds, doing the laundry, tidying toys, sweeping the kitchen floor, wiping kitchen surfaces, and emptying trash cans.

I know many young mums won't be able to afford a cleaning service and this can be frustrating. And there are times when you would not have access to any help and just need to put your big girl pants on and get on with it.

Give yourself permission to try it if you can afford it. Who knows, it might be the thing that makes a massive difference in your home and family.

Prepare Extra Food

You don't always have to cook fancy or complicated meals just good food with fresh ingredients. — Julia Child

Menu planning is one key to getting dinner on the table quickly. It also greatly reduces stress on weeknights. One of the best purchases we ever made for our house was a medium-sized deep freezer that we keep in the conservatory. Whenever I cook soup, stews, or rice, I make extra and apportion it into disposable bowls which I then freeze. By doing this, we have choices to microwave a quick lunch or dinner later in the week or even the next week. This means I can have dinner ready in a flash on a hectic night, when I'm running late or just want an easy dinner. I usually prepare sauces and stews for the children's food on a weekly basis, so the nanny can defrost the foodstuff in the morning.

Occasionally, I'll spend a few hours cooking solely for freezer meals and stocking up. It stops the temptation of getting takeaways too, so that's good for the budget.

On the flip side, don't be too hard on yourself or feel guilty if you order a take-out or go out for a meal a couple of times a week. If it is going to help keep you and your family happy and sane, go for it.

Become a Queen of Delegation

You can do anything but not everything. — David Allen

Many mothers can get so busy tidying up, breastfeeding, changing nappies, running after toddlers, potty training, helping with homework that they often lose sight of their long term goals. This is not to say we are above the daily household tasks, infact it is a blessing to serve our families. On the other hand, long term financial planning, family traditions, celebrations, holiday planning, and discipline can fall by the wayside if we don't specifically prioritize them. A mother does not have to be a slave to run her home effectively. You want to avoid constantly being in survival and fire-fighting mode. Smart women set up good systems, delegate projects and outsource tasks they don't have time for, as this frees them up to spend time on the things they love, like being with their family or pursuing a personal passion. As a working mum, you will need help; accept it without feeling guilty about it.

My husband usually takes our eldest son to Saturday morning football or music class. This benefits me, as I can catch up on tidying, spend one-on-one time with our youngest son, or even manage a long soak in the bath. My husband does most of the cleaning and homework whilst I do the cooking. In the first instance, enlist the help of your husband in doing the house chores and running errands. Your children can join in when they're old enough.

The important thing is to help your family understand that cleaning, cooking and running errands are not just mummy's responsibilities.

Involve Children in Chores

It hurts both yourself and your children if you don't require them from a very young age to carry their own weight around the house. There are so many benefits in getting the children involved with doing chores and helping around the house. Giving your child a specific age-appropriate job or a specific area in the house to maintain will help them learn how to be responsible. It will provide them with life skills that will benefit them far into their future. These will be the life skills that schools don't necessarily teach, so it is something us parents need to teach our children before they leave home and what better time to start than when they are young. You can start them within the confines of their bedroom or keeping their toys in order, for example. Including the children' in errands to the grocery store or mall is a great way to cross off items from your to-do list while having quality family time together. Always take your child's specific abilities and maturity level into account when assigning chores. I created a sample list of age-appropriate chores that most children within different age groups should be able to undertake. You can find it in the appendix.

Simplicity is the soul of efficiency

To save time, organize your life so everything is near. My children attend the swim school and music classes closest to our house. I get my nails done opposite our house, plus I usually get the hairdresser to come over to do my hair. Use your commute time to fit in the little things you love like reading or listening to podcasts and audiobooks; in my case, its reading and blogging.

Turn off the TV. Sometimes you have to limit TV time to stay focused and productive. The background noise of a TV can be distracting and slow you down. Remember you don't always have to answer the phone, especially when you're in the middle of your high priority tasks. If the call is important, the person on the other end of the phone will call back. Set an allotted time to respond to calls and texts.

Some days your work will take over, other days your children will. There will be times when your children need your full attention, so you absolutely can't do anything else. Stay calm. Less important things can wait. Your children's needs should always come first; keep this in mind when planning your schedule and trying to juggle everything.

Declutter your home

Clutter in your physical surroundings will clutter your mind and spirit.
Regardless of how much stuff we have, we can all benefit from decluttering—

getting rid of things we no longer need or things we haven't seen or used in a long while. The idea of living a simplified, uncluttered life with less stuff to clean, less debt, less to organize, less stress, a surplus of money, and more energy for our greatest passions should sound attractive to everyone.

When your home is filled with clutter, trying to tackle the mountain of stuff can be overwhelming. Many of us begin to feel anxious and defeated regarding the idea of decluttering. However, the journey doesn't need to be as painful as some make it out to be. In fact, there are a variety of experts who have come up with some fun and creative ways to get started.

Teach your children where things belong so they know where things go. Start teaching them the habit of 'a place for everything and everything in its place'. Doing this will go a long way to keeping your house tidy and uncluttered. Of course, they won't learn overnight so you'll need to be patient with them and gently guide them until they've got it. Better still, set the example for them and get into the habit yourself. Here are some quick decluttering tips:

- Store similar items together.
- Throw away old cosmetics.
- Keep closets organized.
- Scan important documents and shred outdated papers.
- Organize photos and create milestone albums.
- Throw out anything chipped or broken.
- Buy less materialistic objects.

Lower Your Standards

Improve your reality or manage your expectations.

If you find you're always stressed and exhausted from continually trying to keep your house spotless or constantly cooking fresh meals, you need to come to a point where you might make a reduction in your standards. Obviously, it's important to be neat and tidy but don't chide yourself up if your house is not always as spotless as you'd like it to be. There are times when a quick vacuum, a clean toilet, and wiped kitchen surfaces will do. Your house isn't on show to the general public, so it's your view that counts. Stop worrying about what others might think of your situation and simply relax in your own home.

Don't sweat the small stuff. Obsessing over little things will have a negative impact on you. Come next week, next month, or next year, no-one will remember or care about that one time that something wasn't perfect. Your children will not remember if they had burnt pizza for dinner every now and then or if the wardrobe was not always well-arranged. Your focus should be on spending quality time as a family and creating lasting memories of fun, laughter, and happiness.

Maintain Your Productive Space and Tools

If you are a work-from-home mum, it's vital to ensure your 'remote' work space is a comfortable, clean, and fully functioning productive zone. Try your best to utilise a room (or even a corner of a room) that is not used for any other purpose. If you work from home, there will be a whole host of challenging distractions, so you'll need to maximise your focus and concentration. My little secret of 'getting it all done' is that I discipline myself to ensure my home and workspace environment is set up correctly.

For optimum organisation, before I retire for the night, I set out my workout clothes. They are prepped and ready to be the first thing I see in the morning. Most of my clothes are iron-free which expels the need of any ironing (a chore I do not enjoy). The comfy trainers I wear on my commute to work are always next to my bed, so I never need to search for them in the morning. I also ensure my phone is charged and on silent, so it doesn't disturb me or my husband whilst we sleep. All of this means I can get ready in the morning in a short amount of time. Periodically I will check all my 'get-ready' essentials, such as mouthwash, bath gel, body lotion, etc., are at required levels. It never helps to run out of such a commodity as toothpaste when you need it most.

MUMMY'S CORNER

What is your top tip for staying organized as a working mum?

It's my kitchen calendar. All our appointments as a family go on this so we have an overview of what's going on and who's away when and what time. I don't always have time to look at my phone, but I always see my calendar when I'm in the kitchen.

Melinda, mum of two

Make lists, and lots of them! If I have a list, I find I am so much more productive because I love ticking them off once they are done.

Emma, mum of two

> Establish a routine you can stick to and do it. It also serves as a guideline for the days things don't go to plan.
> **Feyi, mum of one**

Investing in Your Child's Future

A good man and woman leaves an inheritance to his or her children's children. Proverbs 13:22

Every parent wants to give his or her child the best possible start in life. There is no better investment of time and money than in the life of a child. They are the future. Putting money aside for your child is a great way to prepare them for their future, and can also teach them valuable lessons about saving and managing their finances. *It makes no sense to send a child to school to study so they can get a good job but not to teach that child anything about money.* Kiyosaki (2011). Investing doesn't have to be complicated and there are many ways you can invest in your child's future. In the United Kingdom, there are options such as Child Savings Accounts, Child Trusts Funds, Life Insurance, National Savings and Investments Children's Bonds, Junior Investment Savings Account, Self-Invested Personal Pension and even Piggy Banks. I have utilised Piggy Bank, Child Savings account and Junior ISA for my boys since they were newborn babies.

Piggy bank

There is no doubt that the concept of saving is one vital lesson every child should learn from a very young age. There are several ways to teach children the value of money and the wisdom of saving for a rainy day. The most basic but effective idea for very young children like mine who are aged five and two is to get them a piggy bank or any form of money storage to teach them that money needs to be kept in a safe place.

As early as twelve months, children can be taught to put coins through the slot and store the money inside until it is full. Once the piggy bank is full, the parent and the child can count the money together and decide on how to spend it. They can also start to learn and understand the value of different coins and notes. As an exciting stimulant, the child can look forward to buying a toy with the money saved. Use activities such as grocery shopping and charity fundraising to teach them lessons in managing money.

Child Savings Accounts

Opening a children's savings account with a bank or building society on behalf of your child is a good place to start and they offer instant access to funds.

These accounts offer a great way to learn how to manage money and help get children into the savings habit. You can set up an account with a bank or building society on behalf of a child of any age. You can continue to control the account on the child's behalf until they are old enough to do it themselves in most cases when they reach sixteen.

So when next your child's favourite uncle or aunt wants to buy yet another toy for their birthday or Christmas, I would recommend you give them your child's savings account to contribute towards their funds and investment.

Junior Investment Savings Account

Junior ISAs are tax-free saving accounts for children under eighteen. With a Junior ISA, your child can take control of their account when they turn sixteen, although they can't withdraw money until they're eighteen. Between these years, they can hold both a Junior ISA and adult ISA, which will boost their tax-free savings for two years. If you're confident your child will manage their money well, a Junior ISA is a good option.

Most ISAs will provide the ability to invest a lump sum or a monthly fee up to the yearly limit. When your child reaches eighteen, they'll get a lump sum as a financial gift from you that they can then put to good use, possibly towards university, a bit extra for a deposit on a flat, or even starting a business.

For example, if you invest £50 a month, your child could end up having £17,000 on their 18th birthday which is the current average annual cost of tuition fees for two years or half deposit on a first-home in the UK.

Other countries would have equivalent child investment options. When it comes to investing in your child's future, putting aside just a small sum of money, even as little as £10 monthly, can really add up.

MUMMY'S CORNER

What is your top tip for investing in your children's future?

My top tip would be to open an individual account for each child and deposit a select amount from your income each month. Do your research and invest your set monthly amounts into a verified and suitable investment vehicle to ensure you do not join the statistics of lost investments.

Tolu, mum of two

Join KidStart. It gives you cashback from most major online retailers, such as Amazon. You link your child's savings account and then your earnings can be directly transferred into it.

Abi, mum of two

Set up an investment account of some sort. Something that can grow their money but which you as a parent don't necessarily have access to. Just to avoid you being tempted when life happens. Do it as soon as you can after your child is born. Aim to start with a small amount which you can increase as your child-related expenses decrease. There are usually information packs provided that contain family-recommended investment accounts in your discharge bounty pack if you have no idea where to start. Otherwise, you can use a website like MoneySavingExpert.com to compare what's on the market and the pros and cons of each account.

Melinda, mum of two

Reflection

- Are there areas of your home life you are not proud of or disappointed in?
- What is one thing you can do to improve your home life?
- What action can you take towards investing in your children's future?

Chapter Five: Work-Life Balance

It is not the shortage of time that should worry us, but the tendency for the majority of time to be spent in low-quality ways. —Richard Koch

The biggest frustration for most busy mums is having enough time. During my transition back to work, I undertook a professional coaching session for maternity returners. The coach highlighted the main habits of highly effective people. From these sessions, it was clear that the top two habits an effective working mum should have are 'time management' and 'effective prioritizing skills'.

The Struggle is Real

Every mum I have ever met or interacted with complains about not having enough time to fulfil their responsibilities. Whether it's a good, bad, or average day, there are only twenty-four hours in one day. Therefore, I spent several months working on this section. I'm a very busy mum and have first-hand experience with the 'not having enough time to focus on what you really want' syndrome. With only twenty-four hours in a day, we are made to feel that our time is 'fixed'. Therefore, it is vital to understand the relative importance of daily tasks and responsibilities as a parent versus quality of lifestyle and family unification.

I have very limited local family support here in the UK, given the fact I migrated from Nigeria. I know how it feels to be under pressure to get everything done within ever-shortening time frames. We all wish there were more than twenty-four hours in one day, whether it's for spending extra time with your children, enjoying tranquil quiet time, giving more attention to your career or business, attending church, volunteering in the local community, new pursuits, acquiring new training or qualifications, changing jobs, or just finding time to do the things you love. The main definitive aim must always be to enjoy the journey of the present moment.

Before I became a mum, time was never an issue; it seemed endless. But if you're like most working mums, you're now constantly on the go; the list of 'life' is never-ending.

MUSHCOW Prioritization Approach

My educational background and corporate career in technology and Information Systems taught me about processes and systems. I studied Agile, ITIL, LEAN principles, Six Sigma, and PRINCE2, created continuous improvement ideas, and then implemented them into various parts of organizations. I have been doing this form of work for the past ten years and I learned that systems really do work and the simplest of systems work even more.

During the last three years, I have extensively researched ways to keep my days organised with a relevance to keeping me sane. I want to conduct my life in an orderly and astute fashion, not walking around like the proverbial headless chicken as I did during my first year as a mum. I still don't have it all figured out and some days I get stressed and even cry from the stress, but within the realms of juggling everything I continue to learn and see ever more clearly the progress and growth I have made, particularly in the last two years.

Because of my experiences, I want to help you manage your time more effectively and effortlessly using proven prioritisation techniques adapted from various software engineering frameworks. Together we can find some time in your day just for you—every day. Bit by bit, we are going to find a way to increase time in your life to do the things that matter most to you.

Prepare Your Exhaustive To-do List

I made a long 'to-do' list today. I just can't figure out who is going to do everything.

Think about your current responsibilities—everything you have to do in a typical week. Ideally, break down all important individual tasks into short time frames—let's say tasks which should not take more than two hours to complete. Office work and sleep are usually boxed off into bigger chunks. Your list should be very detailed and cover all family needs, hobbies, necessities, and interests, however big or small. Look at grouping similar activities together into your time frames to help clarify how much of your week is spent doing certain things.

You could likely end up with a super long list:

1. Grab a pen and piece of paper or, ideally, use my blank_to-do-list template in the appendix. The Comment section on the template will be useful later in your analysis.
2. Write down everything you can think of that you do in a typical week.
3. Assign a number to each item on your list.

Below are some items from my weekly to-do list. You might choose ones that apply to you and add them to your list.

1. Quiet time and devotion
2. Meal planning
3. Cooking for the family
4. Cleaning the house
5. Going to work
6. Commuting
7. Paying bills
8. Tidying up
9. Doing school runs
10. Helping with the children' homework
11. Overseeing kid projects and activities
12. Children's bath time
13. Bedtime routine
14. Laundry and Ironing
15. Grocery shopping
16. Organising holidays
17. Organising birthday parties
18. Taking children to activities

19. Doctors' appointments
20. Clearing out the shed
21. Sleep
22. Attending school events and parents evening
23. Attending church service and events
24. Planning family day outs
25. Phoning Mum, Dad, and siblings
26. Upgrading the driveway
27. Exercising
28. Watching TV
29. Writing blog posts for *Peacockscanfly*
30. Social media posting and engagement
31. Attending networking events
32. Meeting up with friends

MUSHCOW Principles

Knowing When and How to Prioritise What Needs to be Done

Time management is a process where you learn how to maximise your time. On one hand, it is about making time for the things you need to get done by cutting back on other, less important things. But it's also about making smart decisions regarding your day-to-day tasks so that you are wasting as little time as possible. Great time management means being effective as well as efficient. Nobody is ever too busy; it is just a matter of priorities.

Prioritisation means the decision of arranging things in order of their importance and urgency. Without getting too technical, the Agile approach, which is used in software development, can help you think about your own priorities and determine which of your tasks or items on your to-do lists are important, which are less important, which are potentially distractions, and which can be delegated or outsourced. Tasks that are both important and urgent (time critical) and are aligned with your values and purpose are the ones that should be your highest priority and the ones that you should really be focusing your time and resources on, such as anything related to food, water, safety, sleep, school, and devotion. It helps you consider the bare minimum activities and tasks necessary for you to create, add value, and align with your overall life purpose.

I find that MoSCoW is one of the easiest methods for prioritisation. The MoSCoW approach to prioritisation originates from the Dynamic Software Development Methodology based on the Agile framework. I have adapted this proven procedure to manage and organize your to-do list more effectively and have chosen to call my adapted approach "MUSHCOW".

MUSCHCOW principles can help you think about your priorities and determine which of your tasks or 'to-do' items on your list are important or *less* important, which are potential 'delegations', and which ones must be done by you.

Using MUSHCOW means that priorities are specific and focused. The letters stand for:

- **MU**st Do
- **SH**ould Do
- **CO**uld Do
- **W**on't Do This Time

Below are possible definitions of what the different priorities mean. It is important to decide what these definitions mean to you based on your personal circumstances.

Must Do

These are the mandatory and critical tasks and responsibilities that you have to do as a parent and employee. They are important, urgent tasks like the ones in the top left grid of the Time Management Matrix and must be done to be successful as a parent. These may be defined using some of the following:

- Life depends on it—e.g. food, water, sleep
- Unsafe without it—e.g. gas leak, carbon monoxide detector needs fixing
- It is key to your minimum parenting standards, values and faith—e.g. prayer and quiet time, take a child to school, ensure homework is completed, attend parents evening

Should Do

These are important tasks, which are not necessarily urgent or time critical, that often have substitutes. Also, these are tasks that could be delegated to your husband, someone else or leverage the use of technology—e.g. cleaning, laundry, and grocery shopping.

Could Do

These are wanted or desirable activities which are required but less important—e.g. gardening, hanging a wall frame, attending a school fun fair, or taking the children to a park.

Won't Do

These are activities you have agreed upon with your husband that you won't do *for now*. It helps keep focus prominent on the important tasks, like the Could Dos, Should Dos, and particularly the Must Dos. The Won't Dos might be tasks such as activity classes you have decided not to pursue for the time being—e.g. our four-year-old son's drama and karate classes and upgrading our driveway.

Analyse Your To-Do List

Most of us have a to-do list that is way longer than the number of hours in a day, so how do efficient mums seem to stay on top of everything? The answer is they do not do everything on their own. They constantly try to ditch time-wasting activities to have a calmer, more organised life with plenty of quality time with their family. The exhaustive task list you documented in the previous section will give you a better picture of where all your time goes and, more importantly, where it's being wasted. Ask yourself the following questions:

- Is there any room for improvement? What tasks are the necessary, important, and time critical tasks that I have to keep?
- Which tasks take too long to do but I can give up or delegate?
- What can I give up completely?
- Which tasks, which do not make me happy, can I outsource if resources permitted? E.g. cleaning and ironing.
- What tasks can I respectfully delegate or pass over to the hubby or any other trusted family? E.g. Children's Homework or some of the children's activities.

- Which tasks can I improve or optimise? E.g. online grocery shopping, Amazon prime recurring orders, dishes using dish washer, or cooking in bulk.
- What can my family do without? E.g. meals that take too long to prepare and cook.
- What distractions can I remove? E.g. time spent scrolling endlessly on social media.
- Which tasks can you reduce time on? E.g. spending an hour with your mum or friend on the phone daily, time spent posting and engaging on social media, or watching TV.
- Which tasks can I leave for now and revisit later? E.g. upgrading the driveway or cleaning the garden shed.

The aim of this exercise is to get a minimum of an hour a day back for your family and yourself. When I did this exercise, I was surprised at how much time I was spending on bedtime routines, watching TV, and getting ready for work. I learned how to reduce the time it took to get ready in the morning by getting organised the previous night. I also paved the way to reduce the time I spent watching TV series like Breaking Bad, Game of Thrones, and Suits to ensure I got more sleep. This exercise also prompted our decision to buy a dishwasher, which has significantly helped reduce the time it takes to clean dishes.

I organised my to-do list in such a way that I could fit in extra tasks, such as post-office runs, lunch-break bank visits, or a little 'pamper me' time before having to pick up my son. Doing this exercise will keep you mindful of where all your time goes and determine what your priorities are and which tasks are unnecessary. I applied this approach to some of the items from my exhaustive to-do list. Delegate in my own case means to pass on or share the task with my husband whilst outsource means passing on to an external party, such as a nanny or cleaner. Some of the tasks were a combination of Keep, Simplify, and Delegate, meaning it could be shared between myself, my husband, and our nanny. Below was the result:

No	Task	Prioritization	Comment
1	Quiet time and devotion	Must Do	Keep
2	Homework	Must Do	Keep/Delegate
3	Cooking	Must Do	Keep/Optimize
4	Cleaning the house	Should Do	Keep/Delegate/Outsource
5	Doing the school runs	Must Do	Keep/Delegate/Outsource
6	Attending parents evening	Must Do	Keep/Delegate
7	Bedtime routine	Should Do	Keep/Delegate
8	Laundry/ironing	Should Do	Outsource
9	Grocery shopping	Must Do	Optimise/Bulk purchase
10	Personal grooming	Should Do	Reduce
11	Watching TV	Could Do	Reduce

12	Phoning Mum and siblings	Could Do	Reduce
13	Clear out shed	Won't do	Leave for now
14	Upgrade driveway	Won't Do	Leave for now

Keep Track of Your Twenty-Four Hours

The next step after identifying your priorities is to allocate time to your daily Must Do and Should Do tasks to determine how you can be more resourceful so you know what an ideal twenty-four hours could look like in a day where everything goes as planned and seems relatively 'balanced—balance being if you have someone, like a spouse, live-in nanny or trusted family, pulling their weight and sharing the load.

I get asked this question from many of my blog readers, my single friends, single colleagues or married friends but without children. I constantly get asked:

How are you able to 'do it all'?

Did having children set you back in your career?

Is it possible to have a challenging and meaningful career without sacrificing self-care and family from your daily routine?

When I returned to work from maternity leave in 2014, my transition period was difficult. I felt vulnerable, I had lost my self-confidence and could barely speak up in meetings. I didn't think I would be able to take on challenging projects and go through the corporate promotion process because I didn't believe in myself any longer and I thought it would impact upon my family life. It was my work mentor who suggested I reach out and connect with other working mums in similar situations.

I was invited to a 'maternity returner's' workshop and it was there I connected with other mums who had recently returned to work. We found common ground in that we all had similar challenges and frustrations. It was a massive relief for me to interact with 'nice working mums' amidst all the fear and defensiveness I was experiencing in my transition period. It was clear we all struggled with work-life balance; our jobs were not flexible enough and working from home wasn't popular at the time. If you left work sharp at 5pm it felt almost like you were doing the 'walk of shame', as it was an expected corporate culture that we should all be working late to hit targets and complete project deliveries.

One of the mums attending the returner's workshop told the group how she had to find a new role in her organisation, as the role she had was made redundant while she was on maternity leave. It turned out to be a blessing in disguise, as she was able to secure a new role in another division and the role offered her new flexibility that her previous role did not. She could work from home two days a week and part-time on a four-day week basis. This meant she could be at home three out of five working days every week. It was upon hearing this that I realised I should change roles and search for a more flexible, supportive team and boss.

If any woman made it, then so can you. —T.D. Jakes (God's Leading Lady)

I applied for an internal role in another department which sounded interesting and sparked my attention after speaking with existing team members. Within a month, I had been interviewed, accepted, and changed to the new department. My supervisor and boss - turned out to be the best managers I have ever had. They both believed in me and were extremely supportive in every sense. They pushed and supported me to get my Project Management PRINCE2 practitioner qualifications and trusted me to lead critical projects, which all turned out to be successful. That same year, I got promoted from Associate to Assistant Vice President. I did all this without compromising too much on my work-home life balance; of course, there were periods I had to work late to meet deadlines, but my organisation skills kicked in and helped me at those critical times.

When a woman is sufficiently ambitious, determined, and gifted, there is practically nothing she can't do.

Yes. It's more than possible to have a meaningful career without sacrificing your work-life balance. Just start from a place true to your personality and lifestyle needs and communicate your intentions to find opportunities and environments that will set you up for success.

I don't believe I have to give up my hobbies, interests, self-care routines, social life, and focused time with my family to have a productive and fulfilling career; it just means I have to organise my schedule, prioritise better, increase my resourcefulness, and accept that some things won't always go as planned. There will be times when your priorities or deadlines change and one task suddenly becomes much more urgent. Be flexible and open to reshuffling your to-do list to reflect this change.

How to achieve a decent Work-Life Balance

Set Your Priorities Each Day

One half of knowing what it is you want to do is knowing what you must give up before you get it. — Sidney Howard

Over the years, I have seen many people (myself included) spend too much time focused on things that don't really matter. Time is the one thing you cannot buy more of, so do not waste a minute! Focus on what really matters: the Must Dos.

At the end of each day, create a to-do list which will include your top three priorities to focus on. Even when you have some extra bandwidth, focus predominantly on those three key concerns. They should be the important items that define your overall value, contributions, and success in your job and home. What really drives you to gain the most value for your clients? Ask yourself: Are you working on priorities that drive the overall goals of the business or are you just spending time on work that doesn't count?

Whilst it's important to scrutinise your day and make use of every hour, minute, and second, it's also key to have some down time for relaxation and recuperation; you don't want to burn yourself out. Additionally, it's necessary to pace yourself to have a long, healthy, productive, and happy life and career.

Likewise, in your personal life, it's important to focus on the tasks which add value to your family. Stop trying to do everything and assuming every task is necessary. I learned this crucial lesson early in my marriage. When we first got married, I prepared a local Nigerian soup that I assumed my husband really loved; however, it took over four hours to prepare! It took me a few years of 'suffering in silence' to realise my husband wasn't fussed about that soup and actually preferred another soup that only took five minutes to make!

Learn How to Say 'No'

When you say yes to others, make sure you're not saying no to yourself.
—Paulo Coelho

Just because you *can* do something doesn't mean it's the *best* use of your time. To be happily operative always, you have to know when to say "yes" and when to say "no". Most overwhelmed mums are guilty of over-extending themselves, not just by doing too much but by doing things they don't find fulfilling. Learning to say "no" to things you don't actively have time for or that won't make you feel like you're contributing in a meaningful way is a virtue of greatness. You don't even have to give an excuse; just smile and say, "No thanks".

One of the biggest time-stealers is requests from other people, be it friends, family, your boss, or work colleagues. A colleague might ask nicely if you can summarise a Microsoft Word document into a PowerPoint slide. Ask yourself if this request is something that should fall on your shoulders; is it being asked as a favour? Could your colleague quite easily do it for themselves? Ask if it is more important than the things that rank very important to you. The most successful people can say "no" without intending any offence and none being taken. When it comes to learning how to say "no", practice politeness but firmness.

Here is an example of a good way to say "no": *"Unfortunately, I have allocated the time to update the shared drive. If you can assist me with that, then I can help you with your PowerPoint presentation."*

Each time someone asks something of you, simply ask for something back. They will soon get the message that your time is equally as valuable as anyone's.

If you do not seize control over the commitments you make, you run the risk of allowing your time to be surrendered to others.

Avoid Procrastination

Only put off until tomorrow what you are willing to die having left undone.
—Pablo Picasso.

During my second maternity leave, I travelled to Abu Dhabi with baby number two for a week-long visit to a relative who lived there. We had the most relaxing time in Abu Dhabi, as my wonderful relative and her husband went all out to ensure we had a great time throughout our stay. A day prior to our return flight to London, I received an e-mail from the airline saying our flight had been postponed until the following night. I was gutted as I had really missed my husband and older son, who we had left at home. The e-mail stated we could contact customer service to be compensated for the cancellation. On returning home, I knew if I put off e-mailing the airline's customer service, the likelihood of me contacting them again within the deadline would be very slim. I had learnt the hard way that any task which can be completed immediately, should be. I addressed the issue the day after my return home and thus ticked off that box. To my greatest surprise, I received a cheque in the post from the airline company two weeks later with a compensation amount three times the value of the amount I paid for the flight. Clearly, procrastination can be an enemy of progress and can lead to losing out on opportunities and monetary gains. Assuming I had delayed and not contacted the airline within thirty days of travel, I would have missed out on the bonus compensation.

The procrastination struggle is real, but it's easily overcome by putting a stop to the habit of putting things off. Instead, get into the habit of tackling a task as soon as it hits your hand (or inbox) and claim the time that gets sucked away by the act of procrastination. I once heard a productivity expert give a talk on procrastination. Her best tip was: "If there's a task you can do in just a minute or two, take care of it immediately rather than adding it to your to-do list. This will prevent many small tasks piling up which can end up overwhelming you." Some days, I find that it's hard to find a few minutes to pick up the phone to make a doctor, dental, or beauty appointment but I have re-focused my mindset to ensure I *just do it*.

A good tip is that I usually avoid allowing myself to binge-watch favourite TV series unless I have completed the important tasks on my to-do list for that day. Preparing my soups for the week and going outside to run 2km makes me feel great and guilt-free about watching *'Designated Survivor'*.

Try Not to Multi-Task

Multi-tasking can be an important part of making it through the day efficiently, if approached correctly. I get so excited when I find tasks that can be done simultaneously; as simple as it seems, shopping for groceries online while listening to Spotify is my version of heaven. Catching up with my mum on the phone while cooking dinner is another great multi-task resourceful activity— and it makes the time spent cooking less stressful.

Another top tip for the 'Super Mum' efficiency strategy is to paint your nails while on a conference call where you are a 'silent participant'.

It's key to highlight that multi-tasking is not usually the ideal approach in many situations. There is no benefit in starting a few tasks and never finishing them;

it's always better to tackle and complete each individually. It's much better to allocate time for each one separately. Multi-tasking could be detrimental to quality completion; you might end up ruining several things at once. For example, if you are trying to help your child learn their words while sending a work e-mail, you'll most likely end up giving only mediocre effort to both tasks. It's far better to arrange your tasks in order of importance and focus on one at a time. When adding another task to your list, think carefully how essential it is that you do it.

Leverage Online Shopping

When it comes to getting your shopping done with minimum fuss, online purchasing is a true convenience. Utilise the mantra, "if it makes my life easier and saves time, I deserve it". Amazon is the most useful online shopping service; in fact, it could be a godsend. I have been able to buy the most unique of requests from this shopping platform. For instance, I purchased a lovely authentic sheep costume for my son's Christmas school play; it was delivered same-day with Amazon Prime, so it took away any stress from me having to find, collect, and make the costume. So, next time you need to get a costume for the book day and you've accepted that you can't be a Pinterest mum, don't hesitate, just go to Amazon or eBay. It would be a perfect world if we could order pedicures, massages, and exercise classes online as well!

Believe me, you can get your priorities done in the time you've got and have some breathing space left to do something for yourself that you enjoy. I followed these practical tips and it has worked for me. All you need to do is implement the relevant system that works for your daily routine and schedule.

MUMMY'S CORNER

What is your favourite gadget or app for productivity?

My favourite gadget is my phone. I do everything on it—shopping, banking, communicating with friends, my news channels, entertainment etc.

Sunny, mum of two

All my online banking apps. I don't remember the last time I walked into a bank for a transaction.

Abby, mum of one

Google calendar and Cozi calendar work great for me. You can download them for free.

Melanie, mum of one

Counterintuitively, it is the meditation app "Calm". When I feel overwhelmed or unable to prioritise my day or week, 10 minutes of meditation makes the world of difference.

Elizabeth, mum of two

Work-Life Balance Questionnaire

Work–life balance is a broad concept that comprises proper prioritising between work (career and ambition) on the one hand and life (health, pleasure, leisure, family, and spiritual development) on the other. Here are some questions I wrote out that can help you determine whether you have a decent work-life balance:

- Do you look forward to starting your day each morning?
- Is your work satisfying or rewarding?
- Do you take at least one consecutive full week of annual leave?
- Do you have at least thirty minutes of 'me time' per day?
- Do you usually start your day in a good mood?
- Are you usually able to schedule special and important family events?
- Do you feel you have enough time for yourself or your family?
- Do you prioritise your to-do list daily and focus on your highest priority items?
- Do you delegate or outsource some of your household chores?
- Do you spend time doing things you love doing and spend time with people you want to?
- Do you take time off from work and do fun activities?
- Do you get adequate sleep most nights?
- Do you find time to exercise, eat properly, and keep yourself healthy?
- Are you satisfied with your working hours?
- Are you able to spend some time with your family after work?
- Are you reasonably happy with your childcare choices and backup?
- Are you happy with your work-life balance?

If you answer "no" to most of these questions, you need to re-examine your work-life balance.

MUMMY'S CORNER

What is your top tip for work-life balance as a working mum?

PRIORITISE. Don't try and be a super woman; give it your all but don't be hard on yourself if you don't get everything done.

Gbemi, mum of one

I try to get into the office as reasonably early as I can, so I can leave early and spend the evening with my kid.

Melinda, mum of one

Be intentional about making sure there is time blocked out (technology and work free) for family. When it's family time, be there 100% physically and mentally. But also have time blocks for personal time for the things you enjoy. That could be a massage/salon or exercise. But have it all scheduled. You tell your hours what to do. This leads to less chaos and mummy guilt.

Bibiana, mum of three

For me, family comes first. Luckily, I am a contractor, so I can take some days off and not get paid for it if I choose. In the balance of things, it's less money but more time for my child. Money is important, but family always comes first.

Abby, mum of one

You can never go wrong with having a to-do list! I work and thrive with routines. I always make sure to scribble down things I need to do and get to it before the day ends. The irony is that this list is never-ending!

Lola, mum of two

Family comes first and work last. My priority is to make sure I am spending quality time with my family. I believe the first ministry that God has given me is to take good care of my family. If I can't do that, I really don't know how I will take care of others.

Melanie, mum of one

I try to approach things in a pragmatic way and I try not to take on too much. Despite my worries and fears, I follow my dreams as an entrepreneur. I'm currently in the process of setting up my own business, which I'm very excited about. It will give me a chance to be a mummy to my girls while working. Having said that, I have tried my hands on some things in the past, but it didn't work well with my family life and I had to give it up. (Again, that's what motherhood is, right? Compromise.) However, that hasn't stopped me from going after other ventures and passions. If at first you don't succeed, try, try again.

Annabelle, mum of two

My top tip for work-life balance is to have a supportive spouse and solid support system, be it caregivers, parents, or friends. Integrate family as much as possible. I sometimes go with my children for speaking engagements.

Tolulope, mum of four

> We have a synced work and home calendar which works as a planner and reminder for all work-related deadlines, school activities, parents' evenings, school trips, rehearsals, games, and parties.
>
> **Olamide, mum of two**
>
> I am often asked this question: How do you juggle so many hats? I always reply saying, "I wish I could answer in one word, but it's been the grace of God and having the right support and understanding from my husband, children, mother, and the children's nanny."
>
> **Jo, mum of three**
>
> In terms of juggling, I try to do things as much in advance as I can. I tend to go with the flow and not get too flustered when things don't go according to plan. It's hard some days but there are times when it's easy. Overall, I just try to get on with things, do the best I can and take each day as it comes. My husband is very hands on as well which helps when I've had enough. I think to successfully manage a home with lots of children there needs to be a co-operative effort from both parents.
>
> **Ifeyinwa, mum of five**

Working Mum Parenting Tips

Be the parent today that you want your children to remember tomorrow.

As I mentioned at the start, this isn't a parenting book; it is a book which provides practical advice based on what has worked for me in my journey as a working mum. I know for a fact that to be a highly efficient working mum it is important to get your children into a structured and clearly defined routine. If you take one step at a time, complex tasks often feel a lot easier. Establishing a suitable routine may take a couple of weeks to do (or even longer), but once you have done so, your life should be a lot less stressful.

Sleep Train Your Baby

One thing I can categorically say is that my life as a mum became better and more rational after my husband and I finally sleep-trained our second son at eleven months. That's when he became a champion independent sleeper in his own room. We sleep-trained our eldest son at ten months, just after I stopped breastfeeding and before I returned to work. Since I managed to 'crack' sleep-training my babies when they were infants, their bedtime routine is much easier now that they are older and they happily go to sleep at 7:30pm. Obviously, all babies are different and some could have a terrible teething period, growth spurts, nasty colic, or an illness that prevents them from sleeping properly. Use a sleep-training method that works for your circumstance. Most paediatricians agree that crying is normal and 'cry it out' methods work well for many families; in fact, I saw on Netmums that many working mums apply this sleep-training method. Whilst there are many other sleep-training approaches, such as *'no cry solution'* and *'pick up put down'*, the 'cry it out' method implies that it is okay for a baby (ideally older than six months and in my case ten months and eleven months respectively) to cry for a very short period (about three minutes) before offering comfort. Try to wait until your baby is physically and emotionally ready to sleep through the night, regardless of their age. Some mums on Netmums suggested putting a baby to sleep in a swing but, in my opinion, that isn't sustainable because they won't learn to self-soothe and put themselves to sleep naturally. In a nutshell:

- Keep Your Baby on a Consistent Schedule

- Develop and Follow a Bedtime Routine
- Manage Night Feedings
- Encourage Your Baby to Fall asleep on Their Own
- The Earlier the Better

Teach Your Children Independence

As a working mum, it's highly unlikely you will be the sole means of your child's entertainment. Teach your child the value and importance of independent play. Everyone will benefit from a baby or toddler being able to play alone for a few minutes. Nurture your children to continually learn how to do things on their own. Resist the urge to take over when they are annoyingly slow or frustrating.

Good parenting does not mean giving your children a perfect life; it means teaching them how to lead a good and happy life in our imperfect world.

Avoid being be a helicopter mum; learn to take the back seat occasionally and let your children learn to solve their own problems.

Make Every Moment Count

You will have to accept that you cannot always be physically present with your children as much as you would love to be. The smart approach is to make every moment you spend with them count. When my son started learning shapes and objects, I would point out the different fruits to him and allow him to choose his favourite ones whenever we went to the grocery store. When we were in the car together and I was driving we would sing his Hickory Dickory

Dock or Little Miss Muffet nursery rhymes. At home we count numbers every time we climb the stairs.

Be Positive and Encouraging

Be who you needed when you were young.

When your child starts school, don't make achieving high grades the entire focus and look out for their other talents and abilities. Give them lots of encouragement and acknowledge their efforts.

Children Learn More from What You Are Than What You Teach

Children always copy what they see you do. Do you want children who are kind, respectful, and hard-working? If so, be that role model.

Many successful men and women today weren't top students. Some even dropped out; think Bill Gates and Mark Zuckerberg. However, they possessed other talents that helped them become the successful people they are today.

Speak *positivity* into the lives of your children. Speak to your children as if they are the smartest, kindest, and most beautiful humans on earth, for what they believe *is* what they become.

Here are some encouraging statements to tell your child:

- You are awesome.
- I am so proud of you.
- Keep trying.
- You did it.
- You're amazing.
- You are such a superstar.

- Keep working on it. You're almost there.
- See, you've figured it out.
- Great idea.
- You handled that rather well.
- You are the best.
- I love you.

Enjoy Every Moment

Life is short. Time is brief. There is no replay or rewind.
My son once threw a complete roll of toilet paper into the toilet and all I could do was laugh at my life, which, by the way, I wouldn't change for a thing. There will be times of chaos and that is okay. You don't need to be a perfect mum and your house doesn't need to always be spotless. A home-cooked dinner doesn't have to be on the table every evening. Give yourself a pat on the back for what you have achieved, however small; you can always hope for a better day tomorrow.

Mums often get criticised for their parenting abilities, but guess what? Who cares? Ignore the nay-sayers. What other people think of you is none of your business and once you start recognising this you'll be a lot better off.

There is no way to be a perfect mother but a million ways to be a great one.
The next time you catch yourself feeling stressed, remember there is not one correct path to follow when it comes to motherhood. All you can do is strive to be a great and fun mum.

Be Spontaneous

There was an evening my husband was out of the country for work; I returned home from work totally exhausted. I decided out of the blue we were eating out that night just to shake things up a bit. I put the children in the car and we headed to our local shopping mall, which has numerous restaurants. We ended up eating at my son's favourite Japanese restaurant, Wagamama. In the middle of the meal, my eldest son declared, "Mummy, you're the best." That truly put a big smile on my face.

At the end of a very busy and stressful day, the last thing you want to do is come home and cook dinner for the family. You can spontaneously decide to take them out to your nearest and favourite restaurant or order a takeaway.

Lowering the Bar

One day my son told me that when he was on the bus on his way to his swimming class with the nanny, some older school children were behaving in an unruly manner. I told him they will probably get in trouble for that and my four-year-old son replied, "But they didn't have a mummy or daddy like I do."

Of late, there is the trend of raising the bar in so many areas of life. We need to feed our children better and healthier meals, throw more elaborate birthday parties, sign up for the best summer camps, take them to the best holiday destinations, and then document it all on social media with a perfect filter to make it all look very shiny and perfect. Sometimes it seems like the bar is being raised every single day, but you don't have to follow the crowd.

Good mums have sticky floors, messy kitchens, laundry piles, dirty ovens, and HAPPY children!

Trying to figure out at what level the bar should be set is not always easy. But when does it all become too much and unrealistic?

I suspect the answer is different for every family and for every season of life. It was my son who made me see where my bar should be at and that was being present.

Sometimes setting the bar at just being there, completely there, is exactly what we need to do. Maybe we don't need to make complicated plans for summer vacations or Christmas. Maybe we just need to sit in the garden while the children blow bubbles and run around with each other or read our favourite books over and over. Even if your family can set the bar higher by throwing those amazing Pinterest-worthy birthday and Christmas parties, don't lose sight of the fact that the gift of your *presence* is what they'll really remember.

MUMMY'S CORNER

What do you enjoy most about being a mum?

I find it quite fulfilling that I am able to juggle both work and family.

Gbemi, mum of one

I adore being a mum just because I have these two boys who light up each day. Yes, there are frustrations and there is sleep deprivation, but when they smile at you or make you laugh it just makes everything worthwhile. They make my life complete.

Emma, mum of two

> I love being a mum. I love the unselfish love I get from the children. It is unconditional. That is what I love the most. To love and be loved equally in return.
>
> **Tolulope, mum of four**
>
> At this stage, my son is only eleven weeks old; therefore, the only thing I can say is when I look at him and he identifies me and smiles; that moment is worth a million dollars.
>
> **Lara, mum of one**
>
> I love everything about being a mum but there are challenging days! But I'm grateful all in all.
>
> **Omolade, mum of two**

Reflection

- How do you manage your daily to-do lists? Are there room for improvements?
- What distractions do you need to cut out from your activities?
- What tools or technology can you leverage to optimize your schedule?

Chapter Six: Building an Effective Support System

It takes a whole village to raise a child. —African Proverb

I live over 4,000 miles away from my immediate family and as much as I tried to establish connections with relatives and friends nearby, I still found that no one else could offer the type of support I needed quite like my mother. Several times I have considered moving back to my country of origin to ensure I am closer to my family because I want my children to grow up around people who love and care for them. No doubt being around family can give you unparalleled peace of mind because you can leave your children in a safe environment with trusted people—especially if you're lucky enough to have older parents who have retired. This intrinsic help from immediate family will allow you that extra time to run errands and increase productivity at work and at home which can only bring rich rewards and benefits.

No one can do it all and, unfortunately, our generation of parents are being conditioned to do everything alone because asking for help is deemed as a show of weakness. We work full-time, manage the household, assist with homework and crafts, and everything in between without hardly ever reaching out and asking for the help we *critically* need.

In the past, people raised children in a village. Village life inherently fostered a sense of purpose, security, safety, inclusivity, acceptance and importance. Where I grew up in Nigeria, parents relied on the community to raise their children. They thrive and depend on one another for practical support and help. They relied on one another for strength when times were tough. Parents didn't get upset when someone told them their child was acting up or somebody had scolded them. In fact, they expected teachers and neighbours to scold their children if they behaved badly in their absence. They respected teachers and saw it was a responsibility of *all* to enforce discipline. Everyone knew how important a role they played in ensuring children were raised to understand boundaries and respect authority. This was a natural and fundamental measure of the village I was raised in.

Today, many of us are missing that sense of community. In this western part of the world, it's not unusual to live in a place for many years without ever knowing your neighbours. We feel lonely, unseen and unheard, even when we're surrounded by people. When I was growing up, that was close to impossible.

As working mums in the 21st century we are very unlikely to experience what it's like to raise children in an actual village but that is okay. However, it is imperative we get to know our neighbours, build strong partnerships with our children's teachers, and identify with other parents who share similar values and who can help, support and encourage us on this journey. The path to a village for everyone is within our control. Help those around you who need help and you will find a village. Become an integral part of something whether it's a church community, baking club, dance class or fitness group. If you don't have family nearby, building a strong and effective support network, both at work and with other school mums and local mum friends, is the alternative way to get the backing you need. Pride seems to prevent many women from asking for help however many people usually love being needed. Why not take a bold step and ask another local mum "I am really exhausted would you be able to help me watch my kids for two hours while I sleep?"

Don't miss out on peace of mind and essential rest because you are trying to be a supermom.

Fathers Are the Most Important Support System

A truly rich man is one whose children would still run into his arms even when his hands are empty. —Ziad Abdelnour

There are still men in the 21st century who don't take their role as fathers seriously, particularly those heavily influenced by African culture.

Many men still struggle with are leaning in at home, sharing the load, and getting their hands dirty with changing smelly nappies, cleaning, doing school runs, helping with homework, and taking the children to activities.

Undoubtedly, children can grow up happy and successful with just a mother or just a father, but we must not overlook the benefits that fathers are more likely to bring. I was born in Nigeria and was fortunate enough to be raised alongside my sister and brother in a stable environment by both my mum and dad. Even during early childhood years up to the age of seven, when my dad travelled frequently for work, he was a capable caretaker when he was at home. I recall one time, when I was five, my sister was seven and we were living in a neighbourhood called Ogudu G.R.A in Lagos. My sister and I had just had our hair cornrowed at the local hairdressers. However, our hair was plaited so tight, so when we got home that evening my dad saw how strained our scalps looked and was unhappy we were put in such agony. I remember sitting on the rug in the family lounge upstairs while my dad took out the cornrows for both me and my sister.

Similarly, my husband is a great example of a good father and capable caretaker. He attended major antenatal appointments with me during both pregnancies. We found out the sexes of both babies together and when we went through the daunting school admission process for my eldest son into reception class, it turned out I was unable to attend one of the school open days because of work commitments. My husband, yet again, took time off work to fill in for us. He's the one who does most of the school runs, activity runs, homework, bedtime routines, and bathing duties; the list is endless. Besides this, he was the only one who could easily soothe our younger son to sleep when he was a baby (which meant it was a nightmare for me whenever he was away on a business trip!). It was no surprise that the baby's favourite first word was "Ba Ba". Our two-year-old knows where to look for Dad at home... working on his computer in the study area. His face will light up when his dad enters any room.

One day, I took my son to football class and missed a side-turn. The next thing my four-year-old said was, "Mummy... Daddy never misses the way". Another day the battery of his toy helicopter ran out and he said, "Let's wait for daddy to come and fix it. If Daddy can't fix it, it can't be fixed!"

My husband gives our boys a positive role model to admire, respect, and honour. Having my husband's support makes my life richer and easier.

It is an undisputed fact that besides bringing home a payslip, fathers are hugely important in their children's lives. There has been a surge of interest in the relationship between father involvement and the well-being of their children. This is reflected in the number of books, reports, and articles, such as the Cabinet Office, published on this subject, as well as the number of websites dedicated to fathers, such as Fatherhood Institute and Daddy Doin' Work. The concepts of fatherhood have changed and there are high social expectations for fathers to spend time with their children, as evidenced by recent workplace provisions of paternity leave and flexitime in the United Kingdom.

Without overemphasizing, there are many good reasons for dads to be involved in their children's lives. When dads are actively and positively involved, their children mature better with fewer developmental problems. It also increases their exposure and broadens their mindset, which means a better, well-rounded child is likely to be raised. In her book *Calm Parents, Happy Kids*, Laura Markham highlights why connection is the secret to happy parenting and why the best protection from peer pressure for teenagers is a close relationship with both parents.

Women with supportive and committed partners backing and helping them at home are usually able to flourish in their career or businesses. Sheryl Sandberg, Facebook COO, highlighted in her book *Lean In* how the most important career choice you'll make is who you marry. She had seen and read cases of many women whose promising careers and business went downhill as soon as they had children because they just didn't have a supportive and committed spouse backing them at home.

My family will most likely continue to be a twofold parent-working household in one shape or form. Knowing that we need to run a house and two jobs and rely on each other leaves myself and my husband to work together as a team.

How Can We Encourage Supportive Dads?

On a family holiday to Greece, my eldest son was three and my younger son a mere six months. One evening, my husband was swimming in our private pool with the children and at some point I took a rest on the lounge chair to just observe my surroundings. I heard them splashing around, playing, laughing, and enjoying themselves and it got me thinking how critical dads are in the lives of their children and how I need to do a much better job affirming my husband as a great father instead of finding faults with his parenting style.

It is all too easy to criticise weaknesses and shortcomings while we should tell them how much they are valued and appreciated. Often, this appreciation and encouragement will disappear in the chaos of busy lives and lead instead to constant demeaning remarks, reproaches, and comparisons to their peers and others. Respect, love, patience, encouragement, gratitude, and kindness builds a thriving and happy home. A person who feels appreciated will always do more than what is expected of him or her. Our husbands need appreciation and praise. Even those who don't seem to be putting their best foot forward will do better if they are encouraged to improve. My husband doesn't sit around thinking how awesome he is when he is teaching our son high frequency words or helping him with his writing, taking him to swimming lessons, or reading bedtime stories. He just gets on with it because that's what dads do. He is investing in their little lives, teaching them new skills, and prioritising father-son bonding time. It's a role to be truly immersed and engaged in. All these deposits make our sons who they are becoming and who they will be as responsible adults. As wives, we can build our husbands up with positive words and remind them how they are changing lives. We can retell them again and again that they have what it takes to be great husbands and fathers, that they are wanted, needed, and loved, and that we support them 100%.

No husband, wife, parent, marriage, or family is perfect or ever will be. We all fall short in one shape or form, but we can tell and show our husbands just how much they mean to us. We should encourage and pray for them instead of bashing their egos or crushing their spirit. We should be part of shaping them to be an effective support system that we need to create a happy home for our children and to make our lives easier.

Here are some positive affirmative words every husband wants to hear:

- You are a great dad.
- I believe in you.
- I am very proud of you.
- I respect you very much.
- I am a better woman because you are a great dad.
- Thank you for leading our family.
- Thank you for helping around the house.
- I love you.

How to Help Get Dads More Involved in Parenting

A good father is one of the most unsung, unpraised, unnoticed and yet one of the most valuable assets in our society. —Billy Graham

There are still many barriers that knowingly or unknowingly prevent dads from being devoted parents. During my pregnancies, my antenatal appointments were during working hours, which meant my husband would be unable to accompany me unless he took time off. Also, the health visitor conducted after birth home visits during working hours which also meant that my husband didn't get to interact with these unless he took a day off. Thankfully, when I was pregnant with our second child he had a more flexible job that allowed him to work remotely from home. That permitted him to be present during the home visits.

The 'work barrier' means many working dads that would otherwise love to be involved in after birth sessions simply can't be. Without a doubt, the UK government is doing a lot more in recent times to reduce these barriers. My local GP surgery, for example, offers some weekday evening appointments for working parents. These services are still limited, however, and evening time midwife appointments still won't be available in the foreseeable future. In general, most natal health visitor relations are made during the 'working' day/week.

In many countries, organizational structures and working culture have been built around the male bread winner model over many years, and whilst awareness and attitudes are changing, these cultures are deeply engrained in the working lives of both men and women making it hard for them to see how things can be different.

Getting dads more involved is still problematic for many mums. Even for those whose husbands lean in, there is the 'psychological load' that is still being carried by the mums.

Elly, my career mentor, a Managing Director and mum of three, says, *"The reality is, there's a lot that still falls on the shoulders of mums unless you very explicitly (and sometimes belligerently) set it up otherwise. Last-minute costume requests for World Book Day spring to mind!"*

So how can we get dads to be a more engaged and involved parents?

Start them early, get them involved in your child's routines. When my baby was first born I was so anxious about everything, I found I was constantly correcting my husband and telling him how to do things better for our baby which put him off. Take a step back and let them find their own rhythm.

Now he takes on as much as me or even more and I have no complaints about the way he does things at all. Bath and bedtimes routines are great way to bond with the children in the evenings when they are at work all day.

Let go of stuff and try not to do everything as a mum. My husband does the mornings. I leave for the office early so I can pick up the children in the evening and he can work later if needed. Because I am physically not present, he has learnt to 'survive' on his own even if I occasionally have to provide virtual assistance once in a while. He dresses the children. I do leave the clothes laid out to save him some stress. He makes breakfast and drops off one child at school or both at the child-minder, depending on whether its term time or not.

He does this four days a week and I do it one day a week. Pick-ups in the evening also depend on which one of us is available. If both of us are available, I start dinner and he picks up, even though he dropped off.

Melinda, mum of two

Seek Like-Minded People

***It's important that you surround yourself with people who get you and push you to work harder than you did yesterday.* —Alex Elle**

Being a working mum can be hard especially with little support around. There will be good seasons and tough seasons. Sometimes we need someone to remind us of what is important. They cheer us up and cheer us on, encouraging us when we feel like we're running on empty. We don't just need anybody to surround us; we need positive, like-minded people (and godly people, if you are a Christian). People who are humble and honest. These kinds of people are a rare gift. They are people we need not only to seek their wisdom and advice but pattern our life after their life. As a point of reference, you can seek out an older working couple with children who are successful and who you can look up to for advice.

We have to push ourselves out of our comfort zone, opening ourselves up for rejection and even judgement. For the village to return we need to practice some openness with acquaintances and even strangers. This will take reshaping the societal norms of how we interact with others. It will take putting down our phones and really seeing the people around us.

It takes courage to accept help from a stranger however don't look at the people around you as if they are self-absorbed to the point they don't care what you're struggling with. It could be that see you and empathise but are too scared to step into your personal boundary and out of their comfort zone. Make it easier for them. Ask them. Give them the permission to help you.

Whatever we do, we can't do it alone. Successful working mothers build a network of neighbours, mum friends, colleagues and lean on them when they need to. If you know someone else in a similar position to yours, look toward supporting each other and don't be afraid to lean on them when it all seems like too much.

I have had to rely on my neighbour's husband to drop off my child alongside their child at the summer kid's club. I have kindly asked my neighbour to assist with collecting my son from nursery when the train was delayed. There have also been many instances when my husband and I were held up at work and my brother-in-law had to pick up my son from pre-school. It's no surprise that people who achieve a good work-life balance have a strong support network they can depend upon, especially for difficult times and in emergencies.

Mum clubs are a wonderful way to meet and befriend other like-minded mums. I met many supportive mums from the baby groups I joined and they have proven to be highly valuable in every sense. Staying connected with like-minded humans is a cheap stress management tool. Sometimes if you're stressed it can be safer to vent to a trusted mum friend rather than venting to your spouse or family.

Mum friends are usually my regular source of downtime. I know one of my like-minded friends will always have something interesting planned for when I'm too busy to make plans myself.

It is important to think about the people in your close circle. Your circle should want to see you win and vice versa. If no, find yourself a new circle. Stick with people who pull the magic, not the madness, out of you.

You want to surround yourself with people who have similar interests, mutual respect and a shared commitment of success. Find people who will hold you accountable, challenge your ideas and believe in your dreams. You don't want to surround yourself with people who always disagree with your ideas, those who aren't motivated themselves or those who feel entitled. I have always been turned off by people who feel entitled since I have been working since I graduated from school.

Asking for Help at Work

Sometimes it takes more courage to ask for help than to act alone.

Most women (myself included) believe that asking for help at work will be interpreted as a sign of weakness or vulnerability. In fact, the opposite is the case; not getting the help you need may be career-threatening. Here are tips on the best ways to ask:

Keep in mind that asking for help at work does not mean surrendering all control to your colleague. It means getting over a temporary hurdle, so you can finish what you're doing and move on to the next task or project.

Be straightforward about what your needs are and be as upfront as possible about your time frame. Let your boss or colleagues know what you need but avoid the temptation to micro-manage every little detail. Try to make your request in person and in private. Don't send an e-mail or call your colleague on the phone, especially if they sit two desks away!

Avoid asking someone for help who will in turn make you feel indebted to them forever. There is no use in changing the nature of your relationship into a superior one. After they have helped you, say thank you. Make sure to let them know how much you appreciate their help.

Asking for Help with Childcare

I recommend writing down the names of everyone who has offered to babysit, either during your pregnancy or after you had your baby or anyone who asked you to let them know if they can help. Most mums need help with childcare from time to time; the trick is to be reasonable about it. Everyone knows the mum who refuses to hire a child-minder and instead asks every other female in the neighbourhood to assist with looking after her children. It's not only unfair to the child but unfair to the other mums too. Where possible, make it reciprocal; "if you pick up Moses from school next week for me, I will pick up Lola for you the week after." Avoid falling into the position of always being the taker.

Pick up on other people's cues. Does your mum friend appear thrilled to have your child over or are they barely able to say yes excitedly? If they don't appear genuinely willing, then there is no point leaving your child with someone who wouldn't be happy or excited to look after them.

Offer money. Many mums work part-time and there are those who are short on cash. If they regularly provide childcare while you look after an important project, why not make it worth their while? If they won't accept cash, a nice gift would likely be appreciated. Always attempt to make it a win-win situation.

Surround Yourself with Positive and Supportive People

If you come across people who make you laugh a little louder, smile a bit bigger, and live just a little better, they are the people worth surrounding yourself with. This quote from Karl Marx summarises it: "Surround yourself with people who make you happy. People who make you laugh, who help you when you're in need. People who genuinely care. They are the ones worth keeping in your life. Everyone else is just passing through."

Every successful working mum needs support, encouragement, and understanding to nail it at work and at home. She needs people with whom she can share her joys and triumphs with as well as her challenges, pains, and fears. She needs people who can give her a helping hand when she needs it, people who may never understand the nature of her work but who will be there to support her regardless.

Make your friends and family a part of your success. Let them know you appreciate them and that you could not have made it this far without them; it becomes easy to get more help and support when you need it. Successful moms invite people into their lives who will not only tell them the good, the bad, and the ugly, but who will also walk alongside them through thick and thin. This kind of friendship isn't a luxury, it is a necessity. If you have a friend or two like that your chances of being successful are very high.

I have had to rely on my most trusted friends to help me babysit my children a few times and it's a great feeling knowing I would gladly do the same for them.

Ensure the people around you and your children are those who provide a positive source of energy and support. Keep at least three good friends that can help you in an emergency and vice versa. A person with three solid friends is very wealthy indeed.

Maybe you have friendship that has grown a little distant or cold. Why don't you call your friend and invite her to lunch?

Find a life mentor or network of people who will encourage you and help you keep going. Whoever these people are in your life, find them because you are going to need them when the challenges of motherhood and life converge and nothing seems to be going your way. When I'm feeling discouraged, I meet with my mentor and she usually put things in perspective and leaves me feeling reenergized.

Many mums use the website meetup.com to find support groups for all kinds of different interests which are baby and mommy-related. Through some of these meet-up groups, you get to encounter great like-minded people and make lasting friendships. I have organised and run several meet-up groups in London for mums and they have always proven to be joyous occasions and successful in achieving good, solid human interaction.

Nurture Your Friendships

Friendship isn't always about whom you've known the longest. It's about who walked into your life and said, "I'm here for you" and proved it.

Friendship is the best enabler to great mental and physical health. Focus your precious time on a few good friends you care for deeply. Check up on them regularly—at least once every week. Listen to what they say and what they want, be engaged and attentive, and be of service to them. A strong friendship doesn't require daily conversations or being together all the time, but it does entail some loving care.

When your friends think you're ignoring them, but your child is really on YouTube and declining calls.

There are times where I am just too busy with work and occupied with my family to keep up with friendships, but I do expect my true friends to understand and be supportive towards my circumstance, just as I would be to them if they were in such busy, stressful periods. If the relationship lives in the heart, true friends never part.

Nurturing friendships is about giving without expecting anything in return. However, if you're a good friend, your friends will appreciate and give back too. Be supportive, real, open, appreciative, and compassionate towards your most valued friends. A true friend is someone who sees the pain in your eyes while everyone else believes the smile on your face.

Buy gifts for your friends' birthdays or even just as a surprise. If they have children, offer to help with the babysitting. Buy small thoughtful gifts for their children for Christmas or birthdays.

Some of the best moments between friends can be when you're just sitting quietly together, feeling the calm, relaxed energy between you and offering kindness to one another, sharing stories, and being playful.

Invite friends over for a movie night or spend an evening chatting in the lounge. Relive funny memories over a delivery pizza or glasses of wine. As you sit back and relax, plan your next exciting endeavour. Share dreams of the future and have fun fantasising.

MUMMY'S CORNER

How do you nurture your friendships as a busy working mum?

Staying in touch with family and friends regularly and giving and accepting help when required.

Funmilola, mum of two

Asking for help so you can take a break to rest or do whatever helps you wind down, such as getting together with friends.

Feyi, mum of two

Why Some Women Find It Hard to Support Other Women

Girls compete. Women empower one another. There is always room for everyone to succeed.

Many women I interact with have complained about this being a challenge. I have some very dear and lovely female friends, mummy friends, and colleagues that have been a great and constant support to me in all areas: socially, professionally, and spiritually. They still are. My close mummy friends have become my biggest support system since I had my children. They encourage, motivate, and even help with childcare when I'm stuck. We also hang out every now and then just to unwind and share notes. I have had one or two bad experiences with women that do not support or are not authentic. It pains me when I hear of women who don't support one another. And it is clear this is a problem that is holding many women back.

Former US Secretary of State, Madeline Albright, once said, "There's a special place in hell for women who don't help each other."

So, let me ask, "How are you treating the women around you?" It might prove wise to look at offering a helping hand instead of a pounding foot. A positive mantra to have is: If you don't have anything nice to say about your female counterparts, don't say anything at all.

The next time you see or hear of a woman doing something courageous or acting to be the best they can, embrace her and tell her how much she inspires you. If you see a woman doing a good job, tell her. If they look fabulous, tell them. Self-empowerment comes from giving out a positive vibe to those around you.

Look around. Find women to support. Throw your weight behind them. Get involved. We should stop ourselves from spilling nasty comments that come so easily from a place of envy or jealousy, which are simply projections of our own insecurities. Let's stop the negativity about how women look or what they wear, if they've gained or lost weight, or if they are a stay-at-home mum or a working mum, breastfeeding or bottle feeding, married or divorced. We have a whole generation of girls who are looking at us to see how we treat each other. Let's show them what the power of being a woman really looks like. Let's open our arms to each other and to them.

Here are some comments relating to experiences with women supporting one another:

It is true. Fortunately, several women have genuinely been supportive of me, be it with regards to my career, relationships, family, etc. I think women are competitive between themselves so they either steer clear when they feel they don't measure up or are fake just to prove they're better. I try to be real and honest and supportive with the women around me, but I pull back the moment I'm not getting anything back (and I'm not talking about material things) because I believe it should be a symbiotic relationship and don't want to get caught in friendships that aren't genuine.

Saude, mum of one

Very right! Women compete, compare, and envy too much. It's so sad! Cut your coat accordingly and celebrate others!

Glory, mum of three

Reflection

- Who is one person apart from your spouse and family who you can call when in an emergency or in distress?
- Do you know who your neighbours are? Do you invite them over for a drink or dinner periodically? Do you buy them cards on their birthdays and Christmas time?
- When did you last arrange a play date with your mum friends?
- Are there atleast one or two women in your life whom you have built a two-way friendship based on trust, confidentiality and accountability?
- Do you usually go the extra mile to appreciate and thank your support system?
- If you are an older mum with grown children, can you find a younger mum to encourage and support today?

Chapter Seven: Self-Care and Self-Love

We need to do a better job of putting ourselves higher on our own 'to do' list. — Michelle Obama

When I was still in my early twenties, I would book a mini-pedicure and massage for an idle Saturday morning, head to Westfield (Shepherd's bush), catch up with friends, or go out for dinner without looking at the clock once. Back then, I took those activities for granted—the freedom and flexibility to do anything I wanted to do. I had a very good friend I met from work and she became my travel buddy. We visited many countries together, including France, Spain, and Italy. On one of our trips to Rome, I wandered endlessly around the Vatican museum as it felt like I was in a completely different world altogether. I probably spent close to forty minutes in the Sistine chapel alone. I was in no rush. Nothing prepared me for how over-booked and inflexible my life would become after having children. I miss the old me. The "me" before the children. I feel like having them gave me everything but also took so much away from me. I day dream about being able to turn back the clock even just for a day where I can order food in and watch TV for the whole Saturday in my pyjamas.

My childhood punishments have become my adult goals:
- Going to bed early
- Not leaving the house
- Not going to a party

I sometimes find parenting too hard. I don't want to be the adult with all the answers. I don't want to be the one that has to think about what is for dinner every night or what the children will wear.

As a busy working mum, you have little or no time to look after your holistic well-being either—your spiritual, social, emotional, physical, psychological, rational, and environmental well-being. Being a mum is very sacrificial and can wear you down mentally, emotionally, and physically. We navigate morning sickness, weight gain, and massive body changes. We give up sleep, personal space, and time. It becomes so easy to get wrapped up in our work, children, and doing what is 'expected' of us that we easily forget the importance of taking time for ourselves.

But how will you serve others effectively if you never take care of yourself? How can you give when you are running on empty?

Self-Care Demystified

Self-care" has to do with anything someone might do for the sake of their own spiritual, physical, mental or emotional wellbeing such as praying, mediating, eating well, exercising, or sleeping eight hours a night. Functionally today, the articles researched seem to focus more on stress management, and often target busy working women often with major responsibilities at home and at work. Self-care strategies attempt to apply structure and discipline to "me-time," re-centering our world around ourselves and looking for hope, healing, and stability from some hidden place deep within ourselves. Self-care is:

- The actions that individuals take for themselves, on behalf of and with others in order to develop, protect, maintain and improve their health, wellbeing or wellness.
- Actions and attitudes which contribute to the maintenance of well-being and personal health.
- Any activity that we do deliberately in order to take care of our spiritual, mental, emotional, and physical health.
- Our daily activities in looking after ourselves and something that we do often or regularly without thinking about it.
- The practice of activities that are necessary to sustain life and health normally initiated and carried out by the individual for himself for herself.

I think it is important to do some self-care every day. It may seem selfish, but it doesn't have to take up hours of your time; it could just mean having a quick five minutes to sit outside in the garden with your cup of tea or glass of wine. I believe that putting some time aside for ourselves has several benefits and, ultimately, will make us better, happier, more resourceful people in the long run.

Why Is It So Important to Take Care of Yourself Every Day?

The Proverbs 31 woman not only knows her worth, she knows her responsibilities to herself. She would not be able to provide for others if she neglected her needs—physical, mental, spiritual, and emotional. She makes sure her appearance reflects her respected position as an influence in her community. Taking care of yourself also gives you the chance to expand horizons, which could be as exciting as learning a new skill or as easy as watching a funny movie that makes you laugh out loud. It's important to constantly learn new things, embrace your hobbies, and discover the world and adventures of life.

Doing something you love or something you've always wanted to try will naturally make you happier. By putting yourself first, you can be your best and pass that on to others. Even taking the smallest amount of time for *you* can help relax the mind and body. This will rejuvenate you and leave you feeling a lot more useful. I use the airplane and oxygen mask analogy where you're always directed to put your mask on first in case of an emergency before putting on anyone else's. You must ensure you are in a position of strength before you can be at your best for those who depend on you.

She believed she could, but she was tired, so she didn't.

Some days it is totally okay to just stop and rest. Leave the dirty dishes in the sink and have a long soak in the bath instead.

Here are some examples of things you can do to obtain a little 'me time'. Some of these take no more than 15 minutes:

- Go for a walk.
- Read something.
- Say a prayer.

- Write down your thoughts.
- Listen to your favourite music or an audiobook.
- Phone your mum.
- Watch YouTube favourites.
- Reply to texts and messages from friends and family.
- Do nothing; sit or lie quietly.

Some of these alternative activities would require more time and planning but are equally important:

- Go to a spa.
- Get a massage.
- Have a movie marathon.
- Exercise.
- Take some photographs.
- Learn a new skill.
- Take a hot bubble bath.
- Have a pamper night in.
- Travel.

Here are the favourite self-care activities for most of my close mum friends:

- Sleep and skincare
- Bubble bath and sleep
- Prayer with another friend.
- Soak in the bath tub for an hour and read a favourite magazine

In this next section, I'll focus on describing the activities that have the most positive effect on my mental health and bring the utmost nourishment to my mind, body, and soul.

Prayer and Fellowship

When life is rough pray. When life is great pray

As a Christian, whenever I start my day with prayer, I am automatically able to find peace that passes all understanding, comfort, and stress relief, knowing I am not responsible for everything that happens in life and that I can relinquish my control to a greater being. Moreover, research shows people who are religious or spiritual use their spirituality to cope with life. They're able to cope with stress better, they heal faster from illness, and they experience increased benefits to their general health and well-being. When you feel part of a greater whole, you are more likely to stop trying to control everything.

I know first-hand that it isn't always easy to find time for prayer. But a woman's spiritual life is as important as her physical one; our souls need nourishment too. How can we be intentional about our quiet time when we lead such busy lives? It's simple; we schedule it just as we do doctors' appointments, play dates, and other important events and routines. Set a reminder on your phone. Get up a few minutes earlier. Leave Bible quotes around the house. Make it part of your every day. You might have to give up an hour of sleep, but it's worth it to be able to focus on speaking to and listening to our Father in heaven without any distractions.

Fellowship in church with other brethren is not just something we try to fit into our Christian life after we get everything else together. Fellowship will challenge us, encourage us, and help us stay accountable.

Additionally, we want to be able to constantly hear when God is speaking to us; therefore, attending church services and programmes is the best way to seek and hear God. When God has prepared that inspiring message for our challenging situation, we need to show up to hear and receive it. Attending communal worship has proven to ease psychological and emotional distress and build social support.

Sleep

Sleep is the best meditation. –Dalai Lama

Getting a good night's sleep does wonders for the mind, body, and soul. Sleep is restorative and healing. When I go to bed, whatever I'm concerned about always feels a little less daunting the next day. When you wake up refreshed and well rested, you'll find you can tackle working mum life with more energy and resilience.

I asked the mums in my mum group which of the following they would choose:
- Get eight hours of uninterrupted sleep every night
- Your house cleans itself
- Food plans and prepares itself
- Someone runs all your errands for you

It turned out that 80% of the mums who responded just wanted uninterrupted sleep.

Sleep is important because it allows our mind, body, and soul to regenerate and renew. Our bodies need time to recharge. Sleep is your body's way of replenishing and recuperating. When you don't get enough rest, you will be more susceptible to colds and illnesses and will jeopardise your overall health and energy levels. Try to get about seven or eight hours of quality sleep every night.

Take a Break

In order to ensure we are not spreading ourselves too thinly and constantly heading for burn out, it's important to be able to initiate some alone time. Gravitate away from your work and family responsibilities to regain some natural latent energy. We need to learn to give the same value to ourselves as we give to our work and home responsibilities. Our body and mind are also our responsibility and if we do not care for them, no-one else will. We cannot be great individuals and parents if we are continually exhausted. Sometimes all you need is some alone time for reflection.

I once attended a late-night concert at Hammersmith Apollo with my mum friends. I was a bit worried about leaving the children at home with my husband, but it turned out the boys were both sound asleep and the house was tidy and quiet when I got back home. On top of that, the music left me feeling more energized and assertive and ready to carry on with my duties.

If you regularly go to bed at 11pm, plan to stop working on daily tasks at around 10pm so you can relax for an hour; take a bath, watch TV, read a book, or do something for yourself to disengage and prepare for the next day.

I always seek to do something for *me*; I go shopping alone (or with friends) or I try to see a movie at the cinema with my friends or go to a nice restaurant where I can rest easy knowing that my drink won't be knocked over by my toddler. The one thing that helps me daily is the two hours in the evening I set aside for myself after I put my children to bed.

Take a Day Off Work and Parenting

Make yourself a priority occasionally. It is not selfish; it is necessary.

There are two things I love more than anything in this world:

- Being with my children
- Not being with my children

I love spending time with my children, as they can be fun to be around; however, there are times when they drive me crazy. Ask yourself the following questions. When was the last time you enjoyed a leisurely brunch with a friend? Shopped for clothing without the impatient eyes of your husband and children watching you? Took a gym class or just went for a long, leisurely walk? We all deserve the occasional weekend afternoon to ourselves, to hear ourselves think and recharge our ever-depleting batteries. Offer your partner the option to do the same at some point. You'll return to the family happier, less resentful, more engaged, and able to focus on what your family would like to do without the longing to be elsewhere.

Make sure your spouse (if you have one) regularly spends time alone with your children.

Too often women, even those of us who work full-time, assume the lion's share of responsibility for non-work hour childcare. This includes night time waking, homework time, and school prep in the mornings. Playing the overworked and underappreciated martyr at home gets you nowhere; it only leaves you more overworked and underappreciated and denies your children and your spouse the opportunity to develop deep dynamics with each other.

Women are already at a significant disadvantage when it comes to equal rights and salaries in our society and we have heard too many cases of this in almost every sector. A relatively equal opportunity home is the very least we deserve.

Romantic Getaway (without the Children)

Getting away with your spouse is truly the best way to re-energise those batteries. Usually this would require a change of environment and a change of daily routine and, more importantly, leaving the children behind. But is it possible and is it a good idea for a couple to spend a romantic weekend away without their young children?

The answer is a resounding yes. If you can secure childcare from a close family member or trusted friend who is happy to look after your children, your children will feel comfortable with, and your finances permit it, do it!

Since I became a mum, I've been on two couple-only holidays: one to Spain for a baby moon before my second son was born and the other to Cyprus for our fifth-year wedding anniversary. On those two occasions, I was very fortunate to have either my mum or mother-in-law staying home looking after the children. Obviously, it required planning on all sides to align our travel times and accommodate all involved, but it was worth it.

Many parents fall into the old trap of, "Why would we ever want to go anywhere without our children?" Even if you're the most loving parent or have the best behaved, tantrum-free children on earth, there's no substitute for spending a weekend alone with your spouse, rekindling a little romance, and remembering what attracted them to you in the first place.

Taking time together doesn't have to be expensive. Cheap options include:
- A night spent at a local hotel.
- Last-minute deals on weekend city breaks.

- Borrowing a friend or relative's holiday home.

Girls' Trip

When you try to make plans with other mum friends and you realise none of you are free for the next ten years.

Getting together with the girls is one of life's pleasures. Sadly, it often gets lost in the rush of work and family taking over your life and time. But going away with the girls helps us remember who we are as individuals; it helps us reflect, appreciate, and be grateful for what we have and it's a time for fun, laughter, and memory making.

I went to Spain on a girls' fitness trip over a long weekend to a sports resort. Those awesome days away with the girls led me to question whether it's selfish to take time away to maintain a sense of self or whether it is of massive benefit. Resoundingly, I concur with the benefits of taking time away with the girls.

Mums need a break too. Want to be a great mum and employee? Take time out of parenting and work.

To make my time away work, I obviously had to discuss all options with my husband. He was, after all, going to be the sole charge of the household that long weekend. A full long weekend away is a luxury not every parent with young children gets, but I knew my sons would be fine, well cared for, and loved in my absence. My husband is as capable as I am and I was pretty sure he would be able to keep them occupied and engaged so they wouldn't notice my nonappearance too much. My end of the bargain was that I did all meal preps in advance and ensured the freezer was stocked with lots of different food. I was worried I would miss my boys and, if I'm being honest, I fell into the trap of being a little concerned as to what others might think of me going away on a girls' trip, leaving my children and husband behind. Deep down, however, I knew it was *my time* and the benefits would outweigh any niggling thoughts and preconceptions.

On a positive note, my husband face-timed with the boys every day and sent me photos of what they were up to. Even though I really missed them, I enjoyed my alone time away. It has been one of my best fun experiences since I became a mum and I still don't feel bad about it!

Here are some of the reasons why, as much as I missed them, I was very happy with this much-needed breathing space:

- It was awesome to pack cute dresses, a gym kit, make-up, and shoes instead of nappies, wipes, snacks, and changes of baby clothes.
- Going through airport security was a walk in the park compared to having to bring the baby from buggy, collapse buggy, test milk, etc.
- I was able to read a book and listen to music uninterrupted on the flight both ways.
- I didn't have to take a child to the toilet or change the baby's nappy or feed a picky eater.
- I woke up at whatever time I wanted as opposed to being rudely awoken by a hungry preschooler with lights splashed all over my face and the scream of "Mummy, I want breakfast".
- I got to have full and complete adult conversations—you know, the ones where you start at the beginning and end when you've both finished what you are talking about—without a preschooler or baby demanding my attention.

- I didn't have to cook or do dishes throughout. I was totally catered for. Plus, I ate my meals whilst hot at a properly set table with no sharing (except our sharing platters!).
- I enjoyed the days with very little to worry about except deciding on where to head for dinner in the evening and what time to meet up.
- I managed to sneak some catnaps during the day; I couldn't remember the last time I napped in the daytime.
- I had a full bathroom to myself and was able to use it alone and uninterrupted. There was no audience or knocks on the door because someone was looking for me.
- I was able to leave my apartment with my roommate within twenty-five minutes of waking up without having to worry about dressing children, feeding them, and packing their bags.
- In the evenings, the resort provided entertainment—a complete opposite to my norm, which is me usually having to come up with creative ideas to entertain the children before bedtime and during the weekends.
- The fitness activities I undertook, such as morning gymnastics, running, yoga, and Pilates, meant that by the end of the trip I was recharged and ready to take on the world.

Whilst I know long weekends away like this one will be very few, I proved to myself and my husband that it's fine. My children loved the treats I brought back for them. Now I'm able to confirm that spending a women-only weekend break with a group of amazing like-minded friends can do wonders for your morale and refresh your outlook on life.

If you can't afford a long weekend away, why not try these:

Spa break. Book a day spa or stay overnight at a nice hotel with spa facilities. Sometimes local hotels have fantastic gyms and swimming pools with saunas and steam rooms and it doesn't have to be pricey. I once had a spa day at a local hotel with my girlfriends; we paid just £15 each to use their sauna, steam room, and Jacuzzi. It was an excellent value for the money and it was so much fun.

City break. Look for deals online, whether you plan to stay in or travel away.

Ladies get-together. Perhaps you could plan a girly get-together weekend around a special event, such as a milestone birthday, concert or long-awaited theatre performance. Getting away from it all can leave you reinvigorated. The key to having a good time is to try not to worry about the children and avoid thinking about any possible problems at home.

MUMMY'S CORNER

How do you take time out to replenish yourself as a busy working mum?

I have some alone time right after everyone goes to bed.
Funmilola, mum of two

I love to travel. I really hope to visit Asia soon —got Seoul on my mind.
Abby, mum of two

I make sure I exercise at least once a week. It not only keeps me in shape, but it also gives me that time just for me. Even just half an hour in a day to think of myself and not a little person gives me that boost.

Emma, mum of two

When I am not busy juggling the many hats I wear, I love spending 'me time' to reflect. When I can get away, I travel alone to places that allow me not to think of anything other than having fun.

Jo, mum of three

Nurture and maintain healthy relationships with good friends whose company you enjoy. Somehow finding time to be social with friends and be there for them when they need me makes me feel special. Again, I don't want to find out in twenty years' time that I have no friends and don't know how to be that fun, outgoing person I was before I became a mum.

Annabelle, mum of two

'Me time' for me has completely changed. I used to do sports and hobbies, but right now 'me time' is an amazing full-body massage, some shopping, and some socialising with friends when I get the chance. Sometimes even just to put the television on and relax on the sofa just for the hour is amazing.

Kelly, mum of one

Holidays! We maximise every holiday period and try to go away as a family to reconnect and recharge. Take it one a day at a time. Be flexible and keep

> an open mind.
>
> **Olamide, mum of two**

Exercise, Fitness, and Health

Exercise is one of the most dependable mood boosters you can give yourself. Even a simple ten-minute walk outside can brighten your outlook. So, don't wait till you have time to go to the gym—get out in the park and walk! The idea of exercising can be overwhelming for someone who barely has any down time. It is important to remember, though, when it comes to physical activity, anything is better than nothing. Start with whatever seems manageable. You will likely be able to increase the amount and frequency of physical activity as you start to incorporate exercise into your lifestyle.

Doctors generally recommend about twenty to thirty minutes of exercise three to five times per week, but it can be a good idea to talk with your own doctor to decide what's right for you—especially if you're pregnant or just had a baby. Unfortunately, we are living in a world where a woman's snapback after giving birth is more celebrated than the miracle of the childbirth itself. Please don't try to make dramatic changes in your exercise routine all at once. The most important thing to remember is to set realistic and attainable goals at your own pace. Most people find exercise as a release for their bottled-up emotions and daily stresses. Classes such as Zumba, Pilates, and yoga will open opportunities for you to meet new people with similar interests. Keep it fun and simple.

Now, this may sound like I'm gently pestering but please, if you take one thing from this book, it must be this: when it comes to your physical health, check your breasts often. Get to know your breasts so you know if something changes. If you don't know how to check them, make an appointment with a doctor and they will show you, or research it online. There is vast information out there to help you put a gentle self-check routine in place.

MUMMY'S CORNER

What is your top tip for losing post baby fat and weight gain?

I always tell my clients on the Lifestyle Change with April, "the journey of wellness is not for a period, it's for life!" Start taking care of yourself before you become pregnant, as this will ease you into being back in shape soon after your baby arrives. Coincidentally, one of the chapters of my new book centres on a healthy pregnancy.

Lola, mum of two

Try to eat as healthy as you can. Avoid snacking and make time to go to the gym.

Funmi, mum of two

I am trying to keep up with the gym three times per week. I want to be a healthy and good-looking mum.

Sunny, mum of two

Nutrition and Diet

A healthy diet is a big part of any successful self-care strategy. Nutrition has been linked with emotional, physical, and cognitive health. Eating a healthy diet gives your brain and physical body the vitamins and minerals it needs to stay well. Small, frequent meals can help prevent hunger (which can lead to overeating). If you are working a long day, make sure you take lunch or dinner breaks, regardless of how busy you are.

Limit fast junk food and regulate your portion size. Don't give up everything you enjoy. Give yourself permission to indulge on occasion. Remember: everything in moderation. Regardless of what you decide in terms of when, what, or how much to eat, the key is portion control.

Declutter Your Personal Life

Why live a life that pleases others but slowly kills you?

Getting rid of the excesses in life that cause you stress and focusing on what is important clearly goes beyond material possessions. Our minds benefit from being decluttered every now and again too. The process starts with recognising what no longer holds value to us and then letting it go. It could involve taking a break from social media or saying no to activities that zap personal energy. It might mean walking away from friendships and associations which no longer add value to your life. Trusting your intuition is very important. When we're no longer on the same wavelength as a friend, the energy flow in the relationship can become draining. We might feel weary or stressed after being with them, so listen carefully to your body and trust your intuition.

Some people in your life will make you feel loved, wonderful, and genuinely special; they will enrich or nourish you, encourage and support you, pray for you, and leave you energised. Others might be unsupportive, critical, judgemental, dominating or disrespecting, or perhaps they're only there through a sense of *obligation*. Some people might only be in a friendship with you to get closer to someone you know. Some might even want what you have. When that person has stopped adding value to your life and you've stopped adding value to theirs, it's time to let go. New energy cannot always enter your life without letting go of some of the old.

Reward Yourself

If your mind is at ease and your body is feeling good, you will be more present with your family and achieve more at work. Taking a moment and treating yourself to a luxury facial or buying those new designer shoes or that pricey handbag can sometimes be worth it. While looking after everyone else's well-being, you should never forget about your own happiness and health. Pay plenty of attention to eating right, getting enough sleep, and having the occasional moment when you just focus on yourself. Remember that you need to look after yourself, and while you're doing a great job of balancing your career with motherhood, there must be some time for yourself. Do what you love to do. In this way, if things get particularly challenging for some reason, you will have something to look forward to. It is so important to acknowledge yourself—you're not a robot. Even working mums need to be rewarded.

Couple Time

My husband and I have a ritual; since we got married, we promised to spend a night away from home at a hotel during our wedding anniversary. We have managed to keep to this ceremonial five out of the nearly seven years we've been married. It always helps us rekindle our relationship and stay connected, despite our busy lives. For our fifth wedding anniversary, we spent four nights in Cyprus at a very beautiful resort in Paphos. Thankfully, my mum was visiting from Nigeria, so she stayed at home with the children, who were four and one years old respectively. We face-timed every day and my mum sent pictures of the children—who were having so much fun with grandma. Those four nights away provided us with the opportunity to remember why we connected and got together in the first place; it gave us the space to reflect on our journey together.

When your favourite to-do things become spending time with each other and raising well-rounded children.

Most parents are working longer hours these days, so we have to be careful not to sacrifice our relationship for the sake of our children and money. A happy, fulfilled, and vibrant parent is a much better role model than an overworked ball of stress we allow ourselves to be at times.

The daily demands of work, parenting, house and garden maintenance, and bills can take its toll on how connected you feel with your spouse. Whenever I go out for a meal alone with my husband, we refocus our attention on each other. Time together with no children, no cell phones, and even no double dates, provides an opportunity to stay connected and reminiscence on our memories. Additionally, it offers time to calmly talk through issues and determine strategies for tackling them.

Top Tip: Please don't rush to call your family or in-laws when you're having marital issues. Immediate family rarely forget who did what, so even though you and your husband might make up, they might remain mad at your spouse.

If you need someone to talk to, find someone respectable who shares your values, someone you can trust who is happily married, who wouldn't be biased, and genuinely wants the best for you and your marriage.

Go on a Proper Date

The relentless demands of a career and childcare can easily take a toll on your relationship with your partner and your ability to communicate well with each other can wane over time. Set time aside, monthly if you can, to go on a real date. It doesn't have to be expensive. If you don't have any family around, find a trusted friend, neighbour, or babysitter to watch the children while you go for a meal or brunch, or sneak out of the office during lunch hours to hook up at a local restaurant assuming you work close to each other. It gives you anticipated reason to dress up and a few hours of uninterrupted conversation can work wonders for your relationship.

Romance and Sex

It takes effort to keep looking sexy, but it is such an amazing way to rekindle passion, relax your mind, and connect with your spouse. Making time for your spouse is an important way to show your children what a healthy and loving marriage looks like. It helps them feel secure, confident, and loved. Here are some quick tips for romance with your spouse:

- Give a kiss and cuddle in the morning and evening.

- Call or text to check in during the day.
- Take time to talk.
- Go on date nights.
- Plan a holiday or a night away from the children.
- Most of all, don't forget to play and flirt with each other every now and then.

MUMMY'S CORNER

How do you nurture your relationship with your husband, despite being a busy mum?

I still try to be a romantic wife to my husband. We have regular date nights and we often take short trips together a couple of times a year. After all, once the children are all grown up and out of the house, we will only have each other. You don't want to find out then that you've become estranged in the process of trying to be the best mum in the world.

Annabelle, mum of two

Date nights! There are so many things competing for both of our times that we find it is most effective when we are proactive about scheduling time to spend together. We also try to make sure we spend the time sharing an experience that is out of our day-to-day norm. For example, we might go to a cooking class or wine tasting.

Abi, mum of two

Socialise with or without the Children

One of the most important things we can do as parents is set an example for our children. By fostering healthy friendships and an active social life, we're showing our children how to value personal relationships beyond immediate family. I found myself desiring to spend time with mums who understand the challenges and changes I face. I still struggle with feelings of selfishness when I have fun, but I make sure to push myself to do it regardless. I've noticed I'm a much better mum when I've been having fun.

Having brunch with your best friend could be the therapy you need.

I had to find practical ways to maintain some semblance of a working mum social life and still enjoy time with my children. Let me tell you how:

- Weekday lunches with colleagues and friends. These have replaced the after-work drinks I used to have regularly before I became a mum.
- Weekend play dates with friends who also have children. It's great if they are about the same age as yours. This way the children can learn to socialise while we catch up.
- Phone calls on the way to or from work. On my fifty-minute commute to and from work, I make and receive phone calls to catch up with my friends, extended family, and social media.
- Invite friends over for dinner. Usually this is on the weekends and, if we're lucky, I can get the children in bed before our visitors arrive.
- Go to the mall for shopping. My children enjoy going to the shopping mall and the younger one still enjoys the view from the stroller while my friend and I chat it up and/or shop.
- Sometimes, instead of doing chores around the house, I reconnect with friends via phone or e-mail while the children are napping.

- During half-term and school holidays, I always plan at least one major children-centred activity. In the past, my friends or I have arranged trips to the London Eye, London aquarium, Peppa Pig World, Old MacDonald's Farm, and various zoos.
- Don't take yourself too seriously. Go out, drink cocktails, have fun, let your hair down. Join classes or groups, be it women's professional networks or support groups. Join in some extracurricular fun.

Ignore the Guilt

Becoming a mum is one of life's biggest blessings, but I do sometimes miss having more time to do other things I love. More time to pursue the things that make me, well, me, aside from being a mum. In my first year of being a mum, I struggled so much with voices in my head that told me I wasn't good enough, that I didn't deserve to follow my dreams, and to be a good mum or people might judge my parenting style or approach.

Some people might wonder why I chose to reduce my working days to four days a week (for a lesser pay), which impacted my career. Others might judge that I have a weekday nanny. Regardless, I had to learn to overcome those voices that caused mummy guilt, anxiety, fear, and made me feel less than the great mum God called me to be.

I read the book *Battlefield of the Mind: Winning the Battle in Your Mind* by Joyce Meyer, which is helping me overcome my mum guilt and negative thoughts of giving up when things got hard. If you struggle with negative thinking, low self-esteem, low self-worth, or mummy guilt, this book will change your life. The book challenges you to look at the way you think and teaches you how to overcome negative thoughts and mindsets.

If you change the way you look at things, the things you look at change.

Fear was also another thing I struggled with in those early motherhood days, but over time I had to change my mindset to see why fear is a good thing. Fear is the brain's way of saying there is something important for you to overcome.

Changing our internal conversation from one of self-doubt, negativity, hopelessness, fear, or even guilt is the first step in finding a path to get what we want. Trust me, it does work.

The working mum life is not for the faint of heart. Everyone, without exception, has problems and challenges to deal with. I constantly worry what my boss and colleagues will think of me when I have to take time off from work for school plays or doctor's appointments. I worry about what my children and husband will think of me whenever I miss bedtimes. I worry about not living up to the standards I originally set for myself as a career woman. A full 80% of working mums feel stressed about getting everything done and one in four of us cry about household-related stress at least once a week. That's a lot of tears.

By practicing self-forgiveness and kindness, we reduce worry and stress that can often cause disease. No one is ever perfect. We all make mistakes. We can only do our best and our best bet is to work through any anger and sadness we feel toward ourselves and let it go.

You need to stop the guilt game that has stifled working mums for many decades. Instead, focus on the positives, such as the fact that working mums' daughters are often even more successful and the sons tend to be more caring. You're going to survive, your children will survive, and things will work out. Stop being scared and enjoy the ride.

Enjoy the little things in life because one day you will look back and realise they were the big things.

There will always be times when you think you can't make it or when you forget birthday parties or arrive late to the meeting. Weathering the storms is something you can do as a working mum.

For every choice, another thing is sacrificed. Mums who seem like they're 'doing it all' are probably just really efficient at doing the things that matter to them without worrying about the rest of it. They don't spend a minute feeling guilty about any of the things they don't do because they know how guilt has a way of robbing both time and energy that could be put to other uses.

Working-mother guilt is inevitable. We've all felt it at one time or another, like when our professional obligations cause us to miss a school play or host fewer play dates, or when we miss the homework deadline; accept the inevitability of it all and continue to strive on.

Children are sometimes very good at playing on a working mother's guilt. Whenever my husband or I don't pick up our eldest son from school, he tells us how sad he was about that, which usually makes us feel terrible. I explain to him why it's important for me to work and how we can do so many fun things when I'm out of work. I want him to understand that as parents we might not always be able to be there.

Working mums often struggle with intense guilt, especially when they first go back. They also feel guilty for wanting to work. If you're in this position, know that studies have shown time and time again that good childcare can promote cognitive, language, and social skills. Relieve your guilt by choosing the best childcare centre, child-minder, babysitter, or nanny that you can afford.

To be clear, guilt isn't always a bad thing. It can prevent you from taking actions that could negatively impact or hurt someone else or damage your relationships with others.

Don't let others make you feel guilty

Guilt is the feeling that makes you believe you have done something wrong, that you haven't adjusted to what is expected of you, and that you need to somehow fix that. Did someone say something that made you feel mummy guilt? Set a personal boundary which makes you aware that decisions you make are not in the hands of others but are in your own. Impose boundaries to prevent that person from bringing up whatever subject matter it was that caused you guilt.

You cannot control other people. You can only control your reactions to them.

Relatives can be trickier. If your mother-in-law makes a negative comment about your parenting style, find an excuse to leave the room politely instead of having an argument with her. You are an adult with the power to make your own decisions; you are free to do what you want, even if other people judge or don't agree with you.

Take time off work to spend with your child.

I travelled to Hong Kong and China for a week for my close friend's wedding without my husband and children. I felt so guilty throughout the trip. I was lying on my king-size bed in my friend's dad's hotel after a day tour visiting temples and monumental sites. I reflected on how much I missed my family. But despite missing them immensely, I was also having the time of my life. The intense guilt that came with the realisation I was having such a great time made me take two days off work on my return to spend with the children. I took them to the play centre, the mall, the park, McDonald's, play dates; you name it, we did it! And guess what? Spending all that focused time with them made me feel much better.

For full-blown mummy guilt, give yourself a break and take a day off to spend with your child. You'll reconnect with your kid's daily rhythms, routine, and personality. If your child is little, you can indulge in activities that don't fit elsewhere in the week, like giving them longer baths, grooming their hair, taking them to a playgroup. If your child is older, let him/her choose the agenda for the day. Whether it's the mall, zoo, lunch, or a movie with you, allow them to lead the way.

If you can't take a day off, pick your child up early for a few hours of play or turn a weekend day into an errand-free one and simply spend it just being a mum.

Accept that you may miss out on important moments.

It's a simple fact of physics that a working mum isn't going to witness every single minute of her child's day. It's okay to be sad about missing out on sweet moments and fun. If you let yourself mourn the things you're giving up by working, it may be easier for you to enjoy the things you're gaining. It's no use pretending there won't have to be trade-offs.

To help overcome mummy guilt, ask your day care provider if you can call them to check in. Explain how this will help you feel *connected* to your children during the day. In my case, my nanny usually sends photos of what my children are doing during the day. A photo or two helps me get through those guilty moments.

Know this won't last forever

Life can change in a blink of an eye. The choices you've made about work may seem like they will last forever, but they won't. Your children will change! They may stop the tearful goodbyes and instead run off without giving you a second thought. You'll stop feeling forgetful because you'll start getting a full night's sleep.

When you feel stuck, remind yourself that things won't last forever. Before you know it, your child will be in secondary school, bringing its own set of new challenges. You may get a different type of job with even more flexible hours, so you can be home more often. Who knows what will happen tomorrow? Stay hopeful that things will all change for the better.

How to Cope with the Downsides of Social Media
What consumes your mind controls your life.

For better or worse, digitalization, technology, and social media all form a significant part of our lives now, our children being no exception. Our job as parents is to ensure it doesn't take over and become life itself. While advances in technology has improved the way we interact, work, and share information, it is not without its problems. The main complication, apart from privacy and safety, is that it is becoming seemingly impossible to put our devices aside. The reality is we are now connected to our devices for almost every waking hour. **Nomophobia: The irrational fear of being without your mobile phone or being unable to use your phone.**

I once mentored a group of twenty-eight GCSE students from a secondary school in London aged fifteen and sixteen during a Speed Careers day organized by my work HR. I was one out of six staff from different divisions (technology, global markets, risk, finance, and HR) in my organization that took part in the Careers day. My top observation was that most of the students seemed addicted to their phones. Without fail, they brought out their phones during every single break; some frequently went to use the toilet to use their phones. Many tried to bring a phone out during the sessions, which is strictly not allowed. Teachers had to remind them several times to put all phones away. One teacher told me jokingly that a student can literally have a panic attack if they don't have their phone with them.

We are the generation whose children are growing up totally immersed in social media and technology.
Along with the obvious detrimental effect on our life and work, not switching off can also impact our well-being. The study of the digital world on well-being has increased greatly over the past decade.

Effects on Sleeping
It is common knowledge that technology has a negative effect on sleep patterns. The US National Sleep Foundation states that 89% of adults admit to having at least one electronic device in their bedroom. Melatonin, the

chemical that regulates sleep patterns, is dramatically reduced when using an electronic device before sleeping. In one study published in the *Proceedings of the National Academy of Sciences*, melatonin was reduced by 50% in those who read on an electronic device versus those who read a book. This meant that it took participants longer to fall asleep; they had a lower quality of sleep and lower alertness the next morning.

Information Overload

By opening up so much knowledge and presenting it to us at our fingertips, the digital age allows infinite possibilities for evil and negativity to spawn and grow at an alarming rate. From the questionable to the perverted, the dubious to the depraved, the sad to the shameful, too much information can be presented instantaneously and transit the globe in milliseconds and all of this happens without allowing society the time to sit back and consider the information or ideas being offered.

Breakdown in Face-to-Face Interaction

A whole family can easily live in one household and yet live like single people. Digitalization breaks down many relationships and cuts into the heart of community. While we can maintain friendships in distant states and countries, digitalization can break down all friendships which are not actively fostered in the digital realm. Looking at people with their smartphones on the tube or train reveals a sad truth: everyone is connected, but only to those whom they choose to connect with.

A person can have 5,000 friends on Facebook but can in fact feel more isolated; they lose connection with their innate human emotions by masking their true appearance and developing an online persona that differs greatly from who they really are.

Gadget-Addicted Child

Most modern-day parents have complained that their child is 'addicted' to screens. As most households have iPads and other devices, more children get hooked and eventually addicted. There was a story about a four-year-old who was seeing a therapist to curb her iPad obsession. Evidence suggests children's acute dependence on gadgets could become damaging to their physical and mental health.

Digital Stress and Anxiety

Digital stress and anxiety is caused by negative interactions in direct messages on Facebook groups, WhatsApp, and other platforms, including e-mails and texts. In a poll by the American Psychological Association, those who admitted to constantly checking their digital devices were 11% more likely to feel stressed. Not only that, but people who reported spending extended periods of time online also demonstrated an increase in blood pressure and heart rate.

Social Media Comparison

Too many people confuse internet popularity with real-life significance.
It is becoming more alarmingly common on social media platforms like Instagram, Facebook, and Twitter for people to compare their 'behind-the-scenes' lives to everyone else's highlight reel. You can end up comparing all aspects of your life to a person you've never even met. Have you ever spent hours scrolling through your social media feed then feel inadequate or even

sad afterwards? When you open your Facebook and see your friend's child get yet another medal in school for their outstanding academic performance, your childhood friend renewed her wedding vows on an exotic Fiji island, your high school classmate launched her million dollar makeup business, your cousin just got back from a Caribbean cruise (she flew first class) and your colleague has a brand new Mercedes Benz. You read on cosmopolitan how a mum got her post body weight only three weeks post-partum. You might be looking with envy at all the accomplishments your acquaintances is accumulating while you feel like you are standing still. Many people have become so focused and absorbed with creating perfect digital versions of themselves that they forget to nurture the real self. Smiling depression is where we appear to be happy, smiling and positive but in reality and on the inside we are miserable.

The pressure of taking the right picture, with the right lighting, with the right filter wearing the right outfit at the right place with the right people is just too much pressure for anyone.

How to reduce social media comparison

It is important for mums to be real and authentic with each other, there is no point being fake or pretending that you always have it all put together. Don't believe most of what you see on social media. Kate Spade's tragic passing is a painful reminder that we never truly know another's pain or the burden they carry. We have become conditioned to project only our best selves on social media and sadly even around our close friends and extended family as a modern way of virtually keeping up with the Joneses.

We try so hard to be seen as idealized versions of ourselves and the pressure eats us alive. You have to understand that so many people are not doing better than you in reality. Some just have phones with good cameras and photo filter apps. Don't compare your unique situation to others because you don't know what goes on behind the scenes. Be rest assured anyone that is posting only their success and victories has surely had their fair share of losses, setbacks and defeats just like anybody that is still living. We should learn to enjoy the journey as much as possible and focus on being the best version of ourselves than the best version of someone else. Appreciate your own life. Practice gratitude daily. Follow people who make you feel good about yourself and those who you can resonate with and relate to their lifestyle. There is no point tormenting yourself by following someone who gets under your skin.

Limit Access to Your Device

While we were on a family holiday in Cuba, where they have extensive internet censorship, as much as I missed having my 'normal' constant access to internet and social media, for once I welcomed the restrictions. It gave us the opportunity to experience quality and uninterrupted family time. It is easy for our phones and tablets to creep into every element of our lives. There are different ways to set boundaries for when you will and won't use your devices:

- Agree to certain times that you will not use any devices.
- Have a device-free place in your home.
- Be selective about which devices and social media apps you will use and when.
- Use the mute options. Turn off your notifications so you can control what you see and when.

Switch Off Before Bedtime

There is a significant improvement in sleep quality when you switch off your devices before bedtime. Think about putting down or switching off your devices at least an hour before you want to go to sleep. Perhaps take it one step further and remove all devices from your bedside table; you may be surprised at the results of this adjustment.

Have a Digital Detox

Separate yourself from the artificial world for a while. Take breaks from your electronic devices and social media accounts. Remove yourself off Facebook for a couple of days periodically. Some days we barely use the TV in our house, as it is a healthy habit to encourage more human interaction. During the school runs I hardly turn on the car radio to ensure I chat with the children. Make a point of not bringing your cell phone or laptop into your bedroom and try to take one day, or even one week occasionally, from using all electronic devices. A digital detox will help eliminate stress and give you time for more worthwhile activities. Plan your time wisely so you are not tempted to open a device. Do something you've not had time to do, take the children to the park, or meet up with friends for an outdoor activity. Ensure you have interests and hobbies such as reading, running or drawing that does not involve screens and devices. When you return to your devices, you'll notice things have continued as normal and you've not missed out on anything.

Redirect Your Focus onto Things that Really Matter

When you redirect your attention toward the real world, you find you have less time and energy to direct towards meaningless activities like social comparison. Focus on meaningful and useful activities, such as playing with your children, reading a good book, engaging in a fitness class, or even sleeping.

Limit or Withdraw Devices from Young Children

There is no point in demonizing 'screen time' altogether, as it does have its place, even for young children. There are developmental and educational benefits to be had via the digital space but too much can make little Jack a dull boy.

What if you already have it all?

When I watched Anne-Marie Slaughter's TED Talk on "Can Women Have It All?", she narrated how she made the decision to go home even though she didn't recognize the woman making that choice. I could resonate with Anne-Marie, as I had just returned to work after eleven months' maternity leave with my eldest son. Even though we were in completely different professions and levels in our career, I remember how guilty I felt about leaving my helpless one year old son with a nanny.

Today, my own sons are still only five and two years old respectively, so I'm by no means a parenting or career expert. However, what I do know about being a parent is that you have to make sacrifice after sacrifice. Almost everything requires a trade-off. To do more of X, you have to do less of Y.

Expecting a baby? It might mean you miss out on a long-awaited promotion or pay rise. You want to go back to work early after maternity leave? It might mean you miss your baby's first step or first words. You want to be at your baby's first swimming lesson? Then you probably won't make that operating committee meeting after all. It's just the reality of life.

Since I returned back to work, I have developed additional skills such as patience, empathy, creativity, and resilience through caregiving and nurturing. I now have a wider range of experience and perspective to bring into my work. I previously had the goal of already becoming a vice president corporate title. Whilst it's still a goal to be achieved, it's taking longer than anticipated. My concerns are still: will it cause unbearable stress for me and my family? Will the crazy workload impact my family life, health and well-being? Is the extra money worth the stress it might cause for me and my family? The corporate world can be merciless to those who want to climb the ladder of success but who can't spend long hours at their job.

We need to re-think how we define our "all"
We need to stop thinking about and defining life in terms of "having it all".
No one can really have it all at once. Instead, think about: What do I love? What do I need to do to be happy? What decisions and changes can I make today that will help me get where I want to be? What am I grateful for?
It's not about having it all, it's about having what you value the most.

Think about and focus on what you've already achieved and how far you've come. Count your blessings. Being grateful will pave the way for greater happiness and success, on your terms. Perhaps where you are today is *your* "all".
I've realized very quickly that the only way to 'have it all' is to accept that neither my career nor my family will be perfect.
I must stop expecting it to look like what I expected it to look like. What if my "all" is working 9-5 part-time four days a week in a corporate organization, fulfilling a challenging role where I engage with senior stakeholders, rely on a

weekday live-out nanny, a nursery, and having the ability to spend most evenings with my children *and* having an hour or two to myself? What if being a stay-at-home mum is your current "all"?

Drop the idea of having it all at once. It is an impossible standard for anyone. I'm happy when I finish work at 5pm and can pick my children up from the nursery, play with them, read bedtime stories, put them to bed, catch up on TV, write, and/or spend some uninterrupted time chatting with my spouse.

Even though I'm not where I previously aimed to be in my career, I'm quite happy with my life. Assuming I totally hated my job, or it offered me zero flexibility, or I didn't like who was taking care of my children, I know I have the choice and resources to change it all.

We need to focus on being happy

If any aspect of your life is not to your liking, find creative ways to turn it around. Understand that your career, parenting, and life has seasons. You can do anything you set your mind to. However, you cannot do it all at once. Accept that it's not all about having it *all* today; more importantly, it's about being happy about your *all*. How about you shift from thinking about "having it all" to doing what it takes every day to build a satisfying and happy life?

Reflection

- What does self-care mean to you?
- How do you currently nurture your mind, body, soul and spirit?
- What self-care practices can you incorporate into your daily life going forward?
- How can you be kinder to yourself?

- What can prevent you from achieving your self-care goals
- What actions can you take to ensure your self-care goals are not impacted?

Chapter Eight: Putting Your Trust in God

Trust in the Lord with all your heart and lean not on your own understanding. —Proverbs 3:5

The echoing of, "Mummy, I'm bored...", "Mummy, please can I have some grapes...", "Mummy, he smacked me", "Mummy, please wipe my bum", and "Mummy I'm thirsty!" all ring in my head as my two children constantly compete for my attention. The tension in the house sometimes threatens to suffocate me and, to break out of it, I lose my temper and shout, "Everyone just sit quietly!"

Many people think I'm always put together, when I'm often a total mess. Sometimes I'm anxious, stressed, irritable, overwhelmed, and totally exhausted.

Do you ever wonder why God chose you to take on such a huge responsibility when you simply don't feel good enough or equipped for motherhood?

Many people tell me, "You're such a super mum". I laugh to myself and wonder how I can possibly be. In reality I am that imperfect mum who:

- Forgot to notify everyone I had changed the venue of my son's birthday party. A lovely parent from my son's nursery went to the previous venue and waited for an hour with their eager child, unfortunately my phone was on silent and in a bag. I didn't see their missed calls and text until after the party. I felt so horrible.
- Attended year three parents meeting as another parent asked me less than an hour to the meeting what time I was arriving for the parents meeting. Thankfully I was working from home, I panicked, cancelled all my work meetings and ran all the way to school only to arrive and didn't see any familiar face. It was then I realised it was a meeting with parents of year three. My son's year one parents meeting was the next day as scheduled in my calendar.
- Forgot to organise packed lunch for a school trip, the entire class literally waited for me (and two other parents) to bring in the lunch before they could leave the school for the trip.
- Ran out of wipes and toilet roll simultaneously and had to use kitchen towels to wipe my son's explosive poo before washing with soap and water.

People might think I am a super mum because I put my trust in God. I rely on God every day to direct and see me through the constant challenges of life. There are some mornings where I'm running late and it is very clear I will miss the train. Then God either delays the train for that extra minute or I get to the office only to find that the meeting I didn't have time to prepare for has been rescheduled.

There are some days where I feel so overwhelmed and tired and I know there is no way I'll be able to cook that evening. Unexpectedly, a close friend will stop by and bring a bowl of home-cooked meal.

God has not failed me. He has never left me hanging. There is always a lesson from every difficulty. There were many times I felt like giving up and then God just sends help and surprises me by turning a difficult situation around. If you don't have faith and a personal relationship with God, you might not understand this, but trust me; faith works. **This is what makes people think I'm a super mum.** I am only perceived as a super mum because of God's grace, because of his divine favour even when I doubt him and myself. I usually struggle more when I don't trust God or speak to him to help me.

I find that when I allow life to get in the way, God is the first thing to go. I always feel he'll understand and skipping a few days of devotion will not hurt. But I get hurt. I find myself more easily distressed when I haven't spent time with Him. My children don't listen. I lose my temper, I'm exhausted, and my marriage gets strained too. Everything points to Jesus being our ultimate source, yet it's so easy to push him away or put him at the back of the queue.

The truth is, whether we are a parent struggling with the challenges of raising young children or a marketing executive with client meetings until midnight, most of us are busy. It's easy to push our spiritual life to the bottom of the priority list when our daily to-dos seem out of control. But we can do it. In fact, making devotional time a priority can help everything else fall into place more smoothly, or at least give us the spiritual and mental resources we need to face whatever comes our way. The good news is, no matter how busy your life is right now and no matter what's making it so busy, there's no reason God has to take a backseat.

I asked God for patience during my first child entering his *terrible twos*. Those were tough times. I remember how my child threw a terrible tantrum throughout the entire seven-hour flight from Abu Dhabi to London. Rather than giving me patience, he gave me another son. He is equipping me in ways I never imagined. Both my children are dear to me and each of them has taught me something new and deeper about myself and motherhood.

When my wonderful nanny of more than three years had to leave, I wasn't sure where or how to start looking for someone else. So, I prayed and God provided someone to step in.

God will not leave us in need. Sometimes it's simply a matter of opening our eyes to a perspective we may not have considered. Sometimes we need to get creative with the resources we have. Don't feel creative? That's something you can ask God for. He will give you the ideas you need. He is amazing like that.

Carving out Quiet Time with God

***But seek first his kingdom and his righteousness and all these things will be given to you as well.* Matthew 6:33**

I can assure you, God really cares about all our little issues. It is usually an opportunity to depend on God when you are in need and to trust that he will come through for you. When you need strength, read his word and meditate on it. The armour of God is something we must put on every day. Pray throughout the day and stay connected with Him.

Spending quality time with God may not always look the way you imagine it should, but you can make it happen. Even small chunks of quiet time with God here and there can add up to meaningful spiritual growth. Figure out the best time for you to read your Bible and pray and choose to set that time aside for God—even when you don't feel like it. Don't give God your leftovers. It might not be a good idea to pray at 11pm when you know you're going to be exhausted by. Give God your best spot.

Here are some practical solutions from me and my close Christian mum friends:

- I spend most of my devotional time in the morning in the toilet or shower when getting ready for the day.
- I create a family devotion routine with the children. We usually do ours at bedtime and the children love it.
- I love to listen to Christian songs on CDs or Spotify in the car. I have several playlists of my favourite gospel artists.
- I write reminders, memory verses on sticky notes and scripture cards around the house.
- I set a reminder on my phone to prompt me each day to fit in some quality time with God.
- I read the Bible with my children, even if they're playing on the floor and don't seem to really be listening. By doing so, I'm setting a good example—and they usually surprise me by how much they absorb when they later read back some of the verses to me.
- I setup my phone on a tripod stand and watch and listen to my favourite preachers on YouTube during meal prep.

- You can purchase an audio version of the Bible and listen to it while you cook dinner, fold laundry, or do other household tasks.
- Set your children up with a craft project or something that needs minimal supervision when everyone plays or relaxes in their own room. Use this time to do your devotion.
- Generally, I have less time for my devotion, so I have to be more creative with my time. As they say, it's quality not quantity. I find my prayer points are more targeted and purposeful these days.

Waking up earlier helped a lot. (And going to bed earlier—no movie marathons). There is no formula for timing of quiet time. But be intentional about giving God the best part of your day. For me, that's early in the morning. Even if the children walk in, carry on if you can. Who said quiet time had to be quiet?

Bibiana, mum of two

Finding joy in the journey

Consider it pure joy, my sister, when you face trials of many kinds because you know that the testing of your faith produces perseverance. **James 1:2-3.**

The one thing every older mum with older children always tells me is, "they grow up so quickly". I am thankful to God every day for my supportive husband and our two handsome boys. I am grateful that God chose me out of every other woman on this earth to be their mum.

One secret I haven't shared with anyone other than my mum and closest friends is that just before my eldest son turned two, I came off contraceptive pills with the hope of conceiving and having another baby within a period of a year. **Man proposes. God disposes.**

We went on a trip to Abu Dhabi after I got off the combined pill and I was hoping we would create a "made in Abu Dhabi baby" during our ten-day holiday. That never happened. **I didn't see my period for another 8 months.** I remember my mum once saying, *"women in the child-bearing age who want children shouldn't be going on contraceptives"*. That thought haunted me for those eight months. I know many women who have waited over ten years to get pregnant and some that are still childless. I would still have been grateful to God for the gift of motherhood, assuming I ended up with only one child, so I don't take these treasures God has given me for granted. Therefore, I try to enjoy every single moment of being a mum because God chose that for me.

Even when we have organised our lives to run effectively, life happens. The children get ill. We lose our jobs. We face a financial crisis. We feel like we are not good enough. We go through depression. Our relationships suffer. It's stressful. It's hard. There are days when I just want to hide in the bathroom with the door locked or find an excuse to meet up with a girlfriend because I don't want to deal with my children for a bit. There are moments where I can't seem to get it together and I think I might be losing my mind. I love my children to bits but when they have days of constantly bickering and fighting, it can be overwhelming. On days like this, I try to find a little joy in the mundane and look for a silver lining amidst the chaos.

Like the fact that my eldest son says to me, "Mummy, I love you", "Mummy, you are beautiful", "Mummy, I love your hair". Or the fact that our eldest son is always looking out for me; the other day he said, "Mummy be careful. Move away from the lifts". Or how protective he has become when he says to his little brother, "Don't hurt Mummy". Or the fact my little son says, "Mummy, cuddle" before giving me a big bear hug. Or how, after he has been naughty, my eldest son says, "I want to pray to God to forgive me". How it feels when I open my work laptop to find a star sticker which I hadn't put there or a lego block in my handbag. How my eldest says, "Mummy, that's Justin Timberlake singing" without realising Justin was from one of my favourite boy bands when I was in school.

It is so heart-warming being involved in the development of your children and then watching sibling love ripening.

This is when it all makes sense.

Focusing on those precious moments and what is working rather than the things that aren't functioning usually helps me shift my mindset. I am learning to practice gratitude every day. I am learning to take those in-between moments to connect and play with my children and husband instead of being on my phone. I'm telling myself to shut down my computer and listen actively with two ears.

There are times when I realised I had too many commitments and I was taking out my stress on my family instead of enjoying my time with them. Children have questions. Children are clumsy. Children have needs. Children interrupt you. Children require mental as well as physical energy. I am nearly brought to tears when I think about how distracted and frustrated I can probably seem to my children. It's not their fault I am busy and overcommitted. It's not their fault my work and interests have me stressed. Often, we take out our feelings of being overwhelmed out on those closest to us who need us most. So, the first step, of course, is to eliminate the stress if you can.

I started to take things out from my schedules which were not *as* important. I made self-care a priority. Instead of seeing my children as a drain or interruption from my 'real work', I remembered that they are my first ministry alongside my marriage. Everything else comes after them. When I brought a sense of balance to my life again, I felt so much happier, freer, and empowered to become a better mum.

It is important to love what your children love. Watch their cartoons. Read their books. Listen to their music. Play football with them in the garden. Play house with them in their room. Learn to love their interests and passions. God created them unique. You, as their parent, are blessed with the glorious and beautiful gift to help them uncover and discover their talents. Embrace this time, for it goes by so fast.

My goal is to make the most of this beautiful gift of life God has given me. I may not find it easy to thank God for how my walls are not as white as I would like them to be or how my bank account balance is not where I would like it to be or how my children can be very naughty sometimes because they are just being children. But I can learn to find the joy and satisfaction in all the little heart-warming pieces of this overwhelming, chaotic, crazy, messy, but blessed life we call motherhood.

For Mums Who Need to Persevere
Blessed is the one who perseveres under trial because having stood the test, that person will receive the crown of life that the Lord has promised to those

who love Him. **James 1:12**

When you come to be a mum, it becomes apparent how many things there are outside and beyond your control. You can't govern your awesome nanny moving on. You can't regulate when your child is going to catch chicken pox. You can't control that other child who bit your child in school. You can't control the train getting cancelled. There are so many unknown variables.

Without sounding overly religious, I don't know how those with no faith cope without constantly getting depressed or even feeling suicidal. There will be seasons where you're pushed to the very limit. When life gets so hard; faith can bring help from the most surprising of places.

Perseverance is failing nineteen times and succeeding the twentieth.

I recall one of those days where it was very, very hard. I rushed out of the house that morning to join the commute into the city with my four-year-old who was going into work with me to attend my work's crèche. We literally made a run for it to catch the direct train only to find it was cancelled. The next train, which had a stopover that involved us having to navigate several flights of stairs to get to the platform, was also delayed. Thankfully, a kind man on the packed train offered us a seat.

On arrival into the city, it started to rain at that final hurdle of five minutes' walk to the crèche building. On top of that, my son became so tired and asked me to carry him. I literally had to fight back the tears because I was tired from having been up the night before until almost 1am doing chores and laundry. At that point, I said, "Mummy is tired too and needs someone to carry her".

That made him pause and he said, "Don't worry, Mummy, I won't disturb you again". From this, I felt a renewed rush of strength, a real example of grace from above coming to help. I eventually got to work in time to find the important 9am meeting I had been fretting over had been cancelled.

You can't control everything that happens to you. Sometimes you just need to relax and have faith that everything will work out.

Later that morning at the work's canteen, I was having a hot cup of tea whilst chatting with my colleagues and I felt very happy again. God had seen me through the minor hurdle and had helped me find the strength to continue. In a nutshell, this is why people constantly say I'm a super mum. It's because of his grace.

Winners are not people who never fail but people who never quit.
My biggest life lesson is you can never put your trust in a human, system, or process. Computer systems crash all the time, trains get cancelled every day, and your husband will fail you sometimes. Your family might not be there when you need them. Your friends might not support your causes. Your boss might not be able to help with a pay rise or promotion. Your organization might not support flexible working hours. But God will never fail you. God has never failed me. He has never left me hanging out to dry.

Trust God to Provide the Strength to Endure
What if everything you are going through is preparing you for what you asked for? I have so many personal examples of when I felt God gave me much more than I could handle. But God never gives us more than we can handle; instead,

God's purpose is to allow us to receive more than we can handle so we can trust him to supernaturally provide perseverance and strength.

When you face challenges, know that they are not sent to destroy you. They are sent to promote, increase, and strengthen you.

Pray over your schedule and commitments before you make them. Talk to your husband and decide to prioritise what is best for your family for whichever season you're in. Remember that it really is a season. It will pass.

Try to say no to things that would overstretch you. Change your mindset. Look around and be thankful for the chaos.

***But they that wait upon the Lord shall renew their strength; they shall mount up with wings as eagles; they shall run, and not be weary; and they shall walk, and not faint.* Isaiah 40:31**

If you are going through hell, keep going. Tough times don't last but tough people do. Your hardest times will often lead to the greatest moments of your life. Hang in there and wait for God's promises to come through from these trials.

For Mums Who are Exhausted

Cast all your anxiety on Him because he cares for you. 1 Peter 5:7

Are you waking up in the morning wishing you had more than twenty-four hours in a day? Are you working, cleaning, cooking, matching socks, doing homework, driving children to activities, or dealing with children fighting over the remote control? Are you wondering whether what you're doing every day makes a difference? Do you feel unappreciated, despite all your efforts?

As much as being a mum is one of life's greatest blessings, sometimes it's simply exhausting. Sometimes being a mum means feeling burnt out and underappreciated. After all, who would know that you had only three hours of sleep without having any dinner the previous night whilst still in your work clothes?

Thank God we don't look like what we have been through
Everyone would see me and think I'm always looking 'on fleek' and put together. Trust me; I am often very stressed, tired, and plain exhausted. Sometimes I walk around the place like a headless chicken trying to juggle too many balls. There are moments when it feels like I'm being pulled in so many different directions that it's impossible to comprehend if I have it all together or not.

The other day I forgot to pack a tracksuit for winter PE class, which meant my son had to stay inside whilst almost everyone else went outside. My son obviously survived this episode, but my mum guilt took over.

God understands whatever pain or struggle you're going through.
But permit me to say: "Mum, you've got this."
After going through some low periods and experiencing frightening degrees of anxiety and exhaustion on so many occasions, I can assure you that you will come out stronger on the other side. There will be light at the end of the tunnel.

God is not punishing you; he is preparing you.

It may seem like it will never end, like you will never have a good night's rest again and feel as though you are about to lose your mind. It will pass. Believe me when I say God will never leave you hanging. He will never forsake you. You just need to ask him. Lay all your burdens at his feet. Cast all your anxiety onto Him because He cares about you. He will help you. He will send helpers. You will smile again. You will gain energy. Before you know it, your children will be all grown up. So, trust in God during these stressful times; ask him for strength, grace, wisdom, and perseverance.

God often uses our deepest pain as the launching pad of our greatest calling.

We can argue that it's just motherhood and historically many mums have had to do all these things and more. But being a mum especially with very little "village" is hands down the toughest thing I have ever done. It is always nice to be reminded that I'm not alone and that there are other mums out there struggling and yet making it work every day and night, possibly winging it, just like me.

For Mums Who Don't feel good enough

Are you stuck in a rut? Do you feel like everyone around you is accomplishing so much and yet you feel like a failure? Are you constantly beating yourself up and thinking that somehow you should be more, do more, be better and you don't measure up in your own mind?

There is generally a lot of pressure to stack up in our society. It can be really hard when you see your friends or connections living a nice life while you are desperately struggling to make progress with yours. Even if you don't feel jealous of them, it brings pressure on you when you see someone you grew up with or in your circle doing much better.

We feel like there is something wrong with us if for example our child still does not sleep through the night by the age of twelve months, our child does not attend an outstanding or private school, we don't make a certain amount of income, or have a certain body weight, or live in a certain type of house or drive a certain type of car or take our kids on holiday to luxury destinations. The list is endless!

In the midst of all the self-doubt, pressure and comparison we tend to totally forget all the wonderful, unique and special things about ourselves.
One of the days I was completely down with the pressures of measuring up, I got a comment from one of my blog readers telling me that one of my posts literally got her through a terrible situation. That was when I put things into perspective. People around you will try to make you feel like you are moving too slow but don't pay attention to them. You will definitely achieve whatever you want just don't give up on your efforts and most importantly don't give up on yourself. Someone out there is counting on you. You are enough just as you are.

- There is more right with you than wrong with you.
- The people you compare yourself to compare themselves to other people too. Don't believe everything you see or think.
- Embrace and make peace with where you are. Telling yourself you are a failure won't make you any more successful.
- Focus on progress rather than perfection. Appreciate how far you have come than how far you have left to go.

- Derive comfort in the fact that everyone has their own path, journey and timeline. Your current situation does not define you.
- God accepts you just as you are. Right now.

Therefore, I raise my hat to all the weary, exhausted but incredibly beautiful and amazing mums out there.

The mums who strive with little or no sleep.

The mums who need a shoulder to cry on.

The mums with health issues.

The mums with suicidal thoughts

The mums that never feel good enough

The mums who deal with terrible tantrums daily.

The mums who battle potty-training.

The mums who have children who constantly refuse their food.

The mums who have children that aren't interested in doing their homework.

The mums struggling with finances.

The mums that have unable to get back into work.

The mums who work non-stop for their family, just like maids, and feel like no one notices.

The mums with four children all under the age of eight who never get a break.

The mums with new-born babies who never get any sleep.

The single mums doing it all alone.

Hats off to all of you. Stay strong and keep going.

MUMMY'S CORNER

How do you persevere through difficult seasons?

It's not easy. I rely on God, family, and friends. We go through phases in life that can either break us or make us stronger.

I choose the latter.

Funmilola, mum of two

When I need to cry, I cry. But I know once I'm done I need to chin up and keep moving.

Tolulope, mum of four

Prayer and praying specific scriptures relevant to my situation help. There is so much power in God's word. Also, having community is so important. Having friends and family you can do life with, be transparent with, and have accountability to, is so important. We weren't meant to do life alone.

Bibiana, mum of three

For me, it's my faith in God; if I can't pray about it, then I listen to uplifting praise and worship. The answer is in the question; it's seasonal—this too shall pass. I usually reflect on previous trials and note how God pulled me through.

Feyi, mum of one

I lean on my faith in God, in both good and bad times, but especially in bad times. I find that both prayer and vulnerability work. Being able to ask for help and lean on friends and family can sometimes be difficult but usually turns out to be the most healing and helpful thing we can do for ourselves.

Abi, mum of two

If you're a Christian, you need God to help you and grace, favour, faith, and comfort. It helps to have a supportive partner and a good group of friends you can trust. It helps to talks about it. Be open; talk about stuff. Trust God and believe that this too shall pass.

Abosede, mum of three

Reflection

- What recent situation has made you feel that you might need to relinquish some of your control and put your trust in God to guide and direct you?
- Can you trust God with your cares and worries daily? Can you trust God with your first ten minutes every day?
- Can you decide to believe that no matter the circumstance, God will never leave or forsake you?
- Do you have a life verse that you can affirm when life gets very hard or you get tempted to lose faith and give up?

Conclusion

The move from working woman to working mum is a difficult change in any woman's life. There is no ultimate training manual for combining work with motherhood and life otherwise there wouldn't be so many inspirational books out there related to parenting and work. You will be given lots of advice on every aspect of parenting from people who most likely mean well but it can be quite overwhelming. If there's anything you don't agree with, listen, smile then do what works for you in your home. Every mum will have to learn on the job so there will be some mistakes along the way. There will always be circumstances outside our control. It is important to admit and apologise where things have gone completely wrong. It shows you care and chances are there is always a way to turn things around.

Making it work on the long term requires resetting your expectations, communicating your needs to the important people in your life, asking for help, excelling at organization and time management skills, perseverance, anticipating problems, finding solutions, approaching problems with patience and resourcefulness, and more importantly acceptance. We have to accept we will miss certain milestones in our children's lives and that's okay; there are many more to be shared for many years to come.

A lot of women try to have it all at once: high paying jobs, more responsibility at work, promotions, and raising children. For many, it simply leads to extreme anxiety, stress and unhappiness. We all make our choices. But we should not expect to have it all at the same time.

I want to be able to make sure I'm getting home in time to spend reasonable hours with my family. We can choose to be intimidated by silly expectations at work, but life is too short. Your young children will be long gone in the blink of an eye. Somehow, in this global and digital world where the internet and social media constantly point you to things to do, places to go, and dreams to follow, the beauty of simply being a mum is completely lost.

I'm still learning how to be more efficient and survive the constant demands that are put on my time. Some days I feel defeated and discouraged and others I feel like I finally got the hang of this professional mum thing. But I figured out I cannot do everything. I have learnt to delegate more, even though I believe no one can do most things as good as me. My husband, after tidying up the kitchen, might not remember to put the leftover food in the fridge, which irritates me if the food goes bad.

But guess what? I'm learning to let it go because I have bigger problems to worry about, like getting to bed early so I can be useful the next day. I have come to realize the quality of my children's lives say in ten years or twenty years rest heavily on the choices I make today.

In summary, and based on the insights from the other mums:

- Follow your instincts and go with what you feel is right for you and the whole family.
- Don't compare yourself or circumstance to anyone. Cut yourself some slack.
- You can do anything but not everything.
- Find good quality childcare and backup.
- Establish sane working hours.

Conclusion

- Set attainable daily, weekly, and monthly goals.
- Develop one new skill every year.
- Prioritise and schedule your sleep.
- Embrace the power of "no".
- Let go of perfection. Focus on progress rather than perfection.
- Delegate. Let others manage their responsibilities themselves.
- Don't be afraid to ask for help and advice from fellow mums.
- Have a "personal board" of working mum mentors who you can go to for inspiration and support when you need it.
- Take time out to nurture your mind, body, soul, and spirit.
- You cannot control everything. Pray daily for God's guidance.
- Accept that your social life will change, but that you can still enjoy it and have some fun along the way.
- Remind yourself that no one has a perfect life, a perfect job, a perfect child, a perfect house, or a perfect body.

If you are having a hard day every day or you are constantly anxious, sad or depressed, it is a sign you need to change something in your life. You deserve to feel good and your family deserves to have a happy mum. If you find yourself frequently resentful, it might mean you're failing to nurture yourself adequately. Take note of the challenging times during the day and plan to make it better—whether it's sharing more responsibilities with your spouse, getting more sleep, or resetting your expectations. You might also need to seek help from a skilled therapist, counsellor, or faith minister for further advice and guidance.

Career success without neglecting family is possible

You have to know what to say "yes" to and what to say "no" to. It might take longer than anticipated to attain your career goals, but you will be happier overall if you can find a decent balance. And rather than striving for constant perfection as a parent and as a professional, you have to accept that sometimes 'just enough' is good enough.

Motherhood is no doubt the hardest but most rewarding job in the world. Too often, all this hard work leaves the mum feeling exhausted. I want every mum going through this phase in their life to know they are not alone and that it is possible to get through this season joyfully.

I created a set of positive affirmations for working mums to remind them how strong they are. Use these words to remember that you are always enough—even during the chaos and the struggles. The manifesto can be found in the appendix section.

I have learned that life isn't always easy for anyone, regardless of background, knowledge, skill, circumstance, or faith. I have experienced and watched close friends and family suffer horrible difficulties, terminal illness, tragedy, and death. I've watched good and hard-working people being treated badly at work or in their communities. Over time I have come to realise not all storms come to disrupt your life, some come to clear the path. Sometimes we will lose something good to gain something great. Although you can never be fully prepared to tackle tough obstacles in all areas of life, you can choose to grow and learn from it.

So, mums out there working during motherhood, clearly see that you make a difference. Most importantly, we serve as role models to our children and the next generation of boys and girls to follow their dreams even when times get hard.

Keep wiping those stuffy noses, change those dirty nappies, pick up the toys over and again, come home from work with a smile, make dinner in your work clothes, teach those high frequency words, keep reading those character books, keep folding those clothes, carry on cleaning out the back of the car, keep praying, continue putting your children to bed again and again, give baths, give cuddles, wipe counters, wipe tears, and all that comes with, well, simply being mum.

On particularly difficult days when I'm sure I can't endure anymore, I like to remind myself that my track record for getting through hard days so far is 100%, and that is pretty amazing.

Successful working mums know not to focus on their failures or what's lacking in their lives. Anxiety and guilt is part of motherhood, but it's the joy we will remember most when the children are grown and gone.

You may be reading this and think I cannot be a successful mum because:

- I always yell at my kids
- My home is constantly in chaos
- I dislike my job. My boss does not value my contributions

Listen my dear sister, it is never too late to get back on course and take charge of your life to design it into the life you have always wanted. Being successful doesn't mean being perfect.

So, who will be successful as a working mum?

A woman with faith, perseverance, resilience, and determination will be successful. We are running a marathon, not a sprint. Steve Farrar highlighted in his book *Finishing Strong* how long races require grit, determination and finishing power. Now is the time to seize control over your life (if you haven't already done so) in order to make it the life you will truly love and your children will be proud of.

References

Doyle, L. (2006), *The Surrender Wife*.

Ferriss, T. (2011), *The 4-Hour Work Week*. Vermilion.

Flanagan, C. (2015), Baby Proof Your Career - The Secret To Balancing Work and Family So You Can Enjoy It All.

Godridge, T and Gallie, M. (2008), *How to Be a Great Working Mum*

Hughes, S. (2005), *Marriage as God Intended*.

Kiyosaki, R. (2011), *Rich Dad's Cashflow Quadrant: Guide to Financial Freedom*. Plata Publishing.

Markham, L. (2014), *Calm Parents, Happy Kids: The Secrets of Stress-Free*

Meyer, M. (2008), *Battlefield of the Mind*.

Pearson, A. (2003), *I Don't Know How She Does It*.

Sandberg, C. and Scovell, N. (2013), *Lean In*: Women, Work and the will to lead. Alfred A. Knopf.

Slaughter, A. (2015), *Unfinished Business: Women Men Work Family*.

Thacker, S., McGlothin, B. (2015) *Hope for the Weary Mom*.

Wasmund, S. (2016), *Stop Talking, Start Doing*.

Young, S. (2007), *Jesus Calling*.

Farrar S. (1995), Finishing Strong.

Thompson, R. et al (2010) Maternal Work early in the Lives of Children and its Distal Associations With Achievements and Behaviour Problems: A Meta-Analysis. American Psychological Association. 136,915-942

McGinn, K. et al. Learning From Mum: Cross-National Evidence Linking Maternal Employment and Adult Children's Outcomes. Work, Employment and Society (forthcoming). (Pre-published online, April 30, 2018.)

Acknowledgements

Without the grace and favour of God, it would have been impossible to complete this book, so all glory must be to God in the highest. I am very grateful for this opportunity to inspire other working mums and women by sharing my career and motherhood experiences on a wider scale outside my PEACOCKSCANFLY lifestyle blog.

I have been on the corporative career ladder for ten years, with five out of those ten years being a working mum. However, that does not mean I see myself as a parenting or career expert. There is no handbook to motherhood or parenting; we are all just having a go and hoping for the best. You can see me as a friend who loves researching and sharing. Even I learn new things every day. Without my faith in God, I wouldn't be able to cope with the struggles and challenges I constantly face juggling work, parenting, and my other interests. This book would not have been possible without the contributions and insight from my childhood friends, schoolmates, close mum friends, mentors, colleagues, and several other mums I have connected with through the *Notjustamum* Facebook group, church, Instagram, LinkedIn community, and other professional women's networks. I have met some incredible mums who wake up every day determined to do their best for their children by following their passions. I learnt so much from these inspirational women who shared their experiences and insights with me.

Special thanks to my great mentor Olivia Onasanya who has supported and encouraged me throughout my corporate career and motherhood journey. A big shout out to Fiona Edwards for being a strong sounding board throughout this season.

Massive thanks to Melinda Barthel and Abby Fagunwa, my supportive working mum friends, who had their two babies around the same time as I did. They both helped review the initial manuscript and provided me with useful feedback that made this book uniquely tailored and fit for purpose.

I want to thank my husband Kenny, for his forbearance and for supporting my late night and weekend undertakings with writing this book after the children have gone to bed.

To my children David and Daniel, who taught me first-hand most of what I know about motherhood and juggling life as a working mum. Thank you for turning me into a strong and inspiring woman.

I also want to thank my mum, dad, sister, and brother who have always been there for me. My mum has always prayed for me and instilled in me the importance of prayer, faith, and perseverance. I will always be grateful to her for imbibing in me the greatest and most useful life tool. A big thank you to my extended family, in-laws and friends who has shaped me in way or the other. Shout out to my Pastors who have been a constant source of guidance and encouragement.

I stand on the shoulders of many brilliant and awesome working mothers past, present, and future.

About the Author

Folakemi Sebiotimo (nee Fapohunda), aka Notjustamum, is a Nigerian-British Christian wife, mum to two boys, home maker, daughter, sister, aunt, friend, colleague, mentor, blogger and fitness enthusiast. She was born and raised in Nigeria and migrated to the United Kingdom as an international student. She lives and works in London, United Kingdom. She has a Bachelor's degree in Computer Science and a Master's degree in Information Systems from Babcock University and the University of Sheffield respectively. She is currently an Assistant Vice President at a top investment bank in London, where she has worked for almost ten years, initially as an Application Developer and currently as a Lead Business Analyst. Prior to that, she worked as a software developer at an IT education company in Sheffield.

She struggled with childcare; self-confidence, anxiety, and mummy guilt when she returned to work after having her first baby in 2013. This led her to create the *Notjustamum* Facebook community, a global supportive community for multi-passionate working mums with over 850 members, comprising of new mums and young mums. She also founded the PEACOCKSCANFLY website, an inspirational lifestyle blog, an outlet to share her lifestyle, motherhood, faith, and career journey to inspire other mums to find joy in their motherhood journey, be their authentic self, and stand out regardless of their circumstance. She is a member of BritMums, Parent Blogger club, and Mumsnet blogger network. She is passionate about empowering individuals to make choices that optimise their personal, professional, and spiritual growth, enabling them to live their best life. To access her articles, you can follow her blog on www.peacockscanfly.com and Instagram www.instagram.com/amnotjustamum.

APPENDIX

Vision Board

Career Goal:	Parenting Goal:	Spiritual Goal:
Health Goal:	Love and Marriage Goal:	Finance Goal:
Fitness Goal:	Social Goal:	Travel Goal:
Self Improvement Goal:	Self Care Goal:	Volunteering Goal:

What quote inspires me?

Notes:

Goal Setting Worksheet

Goal Statement: (Specific, Measurable, Achievable, Relevant, and Time Bound)

Why is this goal important?

What steps do I need to achieve this goal?

PROBLEMS AND OBSTACLES
What are the potential problems and obstacles that might prevent me from accomplishing my goal?

Number	Problems or Obstacles	Solution and Action Item	Mitigation date
1			
2			
3			

ACTION PLAN
List at least 4 action items or tasks that can help you achieve your goal. Assign a target date, preferably weekly or monthly to tasks. You can choose to delegate or outsource some tasks.

Number	Action Item or Task	Owner	Target date	Completed Date
1				
2				
3				
4				

How will I reward myself after I have completed my goal?

Weekly To-Do List

Write down everything you normally do in a typical week. E.g. Household chores, school drop-off, school pick-up, homework, laundry, meal prep, grocery, etc. Be as detailed as possible.

Number	Item	Comment
1		
2		
3		
4		
5		
6		
7		
8		
9		
10		
11		
12		
13		
14		
15		
16		
17		
18		
19		
20		
21		
22		
23		
24		
25		
26		
27		
28		
29		
30		

Daily Planner

Date:

What am I grateful for?

Top Three Priorities for Today:

Top Three Priorities for Tomorrow:

Schedule	
AM	5:00
	6:00
	7:00
	8:00
	9:00
	10:00
	11:00
PM	12:00
	1:00
	2:00
	3:00
	4:00
	5:00
	6:00
	7:00
	8:00
	9:00
	10:00
	11:00

Age Appropriate Chores (Example)

TODDLER AGE 2-3

- Pick up and put away toys.
- Stack books on shelf.
- Collect dirty clothes.
- Throw thrash away in the bin.
- Put clothes away.
- Fetch nappies, wipes, phone, remote control.
- Charge mobile phone.
- Put clothes in drawer.
- Dress themselves.
- Assist with light dusting.
- Carry plates to sink after meal.

PRESCHOOL 4-5

- All previous chores.
- Clear dishes after meals.
- Make own bed with supervision.
- Assist with laundry and folding clothes.
- Arrange books on a bookshelf.
- Bring shopping from car into the house.
- Assist with loading and unloading dishwasher.
- Wipe up spills
- Take out bin.
- Clean toilet seat.
- Feed Pets
- Water houseplants

AGE 6-8

- All previous chores.
- Prepare simple snacks.
- Wipe surfaces and counters.
- Unload dishwasher or wash dishes.
- Water plants and flowers.
- Make bed.
- Sweep with small broom or vacuum.
- Wipe bathroom and kitchen sinks.
- Fold Towels.
- Dust Furniture
- Hang out laundry.
- Clean microwave.
- Rake weeds.

AGE 9-11

- All previous chores.
- Vacuum rugs.
- Sweep and mop floor.
- Prepare simple meals.
- Clean bathroom.
- Change light bulbs.
- Wash car.
- Help with younger siblings.
- Take garbage and recycling out.
- Ironing.
- Organise play room.
- Mend buttons
- Supervise younger siblings

The Notjustamum Manifesto

- Everything I do serves a purpose for me and my family
- I am an incredible role model for my children and young adults
- I have survived this challenge before and I will do it again.
- I will nurture myself so I can nurture my family
- I am exactly who and what my children needs
- The decisions and choices made by other mums do not need to dictate mine
- I am raising independent, well-rounded and resilient children
- I will run my own race the best way I can
- I can be a hot mess and still be an awesome mum
- I have the ability to solve any problem I face
- It doesn't matter how slowly I go as long as I do not give up
- I will not try to impress or compare myself to anyone

Printed in Great Britain
by Amazon